LOUIS VUITTON JAPAN

THE BUILDING OF LUXURY

©2004 Assouline Publishing
601 West 26th Street, 18th Floor
New York, NY 10001, USA
www.assouline.com

ISBN : 2 84323 618 5

Printing by RR Donnelley (United States)

Kyojiro Hata

LOUIS VUITTON JAPAN

THE BUILDING OF LUXURY

ASSOULINE

Contents

"The brand business encompasses the essence of all businesses."

My first encounter with Louis Vuitton

It all began with a lunch at a private club next to the Japanese ambassador's residence in Paris on February 9, 1976.

I was in Paris as a member of a research commission organized by the Japan Information Processing Development Institute, when Frank Doran invited me to lunch.

Frank had been one of my colleagues when I worked as a consultant in New York, and it had been a while since we had last met. He had been assigned to conduct an executive search for Louis Vuitton in France.

That lunch with Frank in Paris 27 years ago led to my meeting Henry Louis Vuitton, which was to be the turning point of my life.

The desire to go abroad

In 1961, after graduating from the faculty of economics at Keio University, I decided to study in the United

States rather than become a company employee. Despite my plans to study abroad, my late professor, Hisashi Kawada, had advised me to get a job first so as not to jeopardize my future. I was determined, however. I had dreamt of studying abroad since I was a teenager, and I had made great efforts to learn English.

After spending a year at the University of California at Berkeley, I joined the Amos Tuck School of Business at Dartmouth College in New Hampshire. In 1964 I was the first Tuck MBA graduate from Japan, and I joined the New York–based accounting firm Peat Marwick Mitchell.

I had been interested in becoming a consultant since being an undergraduate student, and Peat Marwick was the only company that hired people as consultants without actual business experience.

I moved to Staten Island, N.Y., and commuted by ferry to Peat Marwick's New York office near Wall Street. After a year of accounting audit experience, I was assigned to the highly prized management consulting department, where I worked with Frank Doran. Frank later married a French woman and was transferred to the Paris office.

Transfer to the Tokyo office

Peat Marwick was the first accounting firm to open a consulting office in Tokyo, in the fall of 1967. I was transferred there, and returned to Japan for the first time in six years to work with an American manager, Jack McCarthy.

Jack had come from the Boston office and was a specialist in management information systems (MIS) for NASA, which at the time was a flourishing sector in the U.S. My main task was as consultant on the computerization of accounting systems. I was fortunate to be assigned to work with Jack, both as his interpreter and assistant on a consulting project on the computer systems of a major Japanese electric-appliance manufacturer.

Jack's experience and knowledge of cutting-edge computer systems at NASA was greatly influential in Japan at the time. The country was being rocked by a wave of trade deregulation, and many foreign companies were seeking a chance to enter the Japanese market. The number of inquiries by foreign companies seeking access to it was rising, and I worked on many of these projects during the 1970s. By 1976, the year I met Henry Louis Vuitton, I already had a great deal of experience consulting for foreign companies wanting to break into the Japanese market.

Frank Doran's suggestion

As we were about to finish our lunch on that February afternoon, Frank said, "One of my clients, Louis Vuitton, is experiencing a big increase of Japanese customers at its store on Avenue Marceau [in Paris]. Many of them are apparently traders, and the Vuitton family is having trouble dealing with them. Kyo [my American nickname], why don't you go see Henry-Louis Vuitton, the head of the family, and tell him about your experience with projects for foreign companies entering the Japanese market? It could be another business chance for you."

I asked Frank to arrange a meeting with him as soon as possible.

At the Louis Vuitton store on Avenue Marceau near the Arc de Triomphe in the 8th arrondissement of Paris, there was in fact an endless line of Japanese customers. Among them were parallel traders pretending to be tourists, buying up a large amount of products. They created a feverish atmosphere, unlike what one would have expected in a luxury store. Uncomfortable with the situation, Louis Vuitton had decided to place a limit on the number of products sold to Japanese customers.

However, I must admit that at the time I had not known the brand name Louis Vuitton or its products.

Prologue

In a corner of the Avenue Marceau store

The meeting with Henry-Louis Vuitton was arranged for the following day, and I still remember it perfectly well. Henry, nearly six feet tall, welcomed me in his office in a corner of the Marceau store, a renowned store in Paris. The serenity and the high ceilings of Henry Vuitton's office were worlds away from my experience.

The long room had a small window from which to view the sales floor, and the walls were embedded with antique trunks. I felt the long history of Louis Vuitton and the depth of French tradition through my body for the first time. It was an awakening for me.

The United States had been the only other foreign country I had known until then. My impression of Henry's office remains in my mind today. Now I have an orange-colored antique trunk inset on the wall of my office, and I think about the first time I met Henry whenever I look at it.

I looked through the small window in Henry's office for a while and watched the Japanese customers in the store. After listening to Henry's ideas about this phenomenon, I volunteered to submit a written proposal for a research project assessing the situation in Japan.

My suggestion was readily accepted, and my professional relationship with Louis Vuitton began.

The creation of a brand business model
Sticking to my beliefs

My first consulting contract with Louis Vuitton

Returning to Tokyo, I was surprised to see groups of three to five Louis Vuitton bags on display in shop windows, even at small clothes shops all over Akasaka, Roppongi, Shibuya, and Ginza. Affixed to these bags were a variety of price tags. I later found out that the prices were unregulated and often three to four times as high as in Paris.

At that time in Japan, the Osaka-based import wholesaler Sann Freres, teamed up with Mitsui & Co., Ltd., was the only company dealing directly with Louis Vuitton. The products they imported through Mitsui were sold in a corner of the Ann International store located in the Akasaka Tokyu Hotel shopping arcade.

That's what I had heard, in any case, but when I visited the actual store, there was no stock at all and nobody knew when the next shipment would arrive.

I soon drafted my first proposal to Henry to conduct research and investigate the quantity and price

Kyo Hata standing in front of the orange antique trunk inset
on the wall of his office.

of the products marketed through parallel importers in
the major cities of Japan—Tokyo, Yokohama, Osaka, and
Kobe.

The research wouldn't be technically difficult, but I
thought it was important to understand the situation
accurately.

I had had many frustrating experiences trying to
convince European companies to use my consulting
services on how to break into the Japanese market. This
time, I decided to divide the project into several phases.
This approach would allow the client to minimize their
risk, because the payment for the first phase would be

small, and the client could then choose to proceed or not after seeing the results.

The research fee I proposed for this first phase of the project was 500,000 yen, plus expenses—an amount that at the time was less than the return airfare between Paris and Tokyo.

This approach seemed to please Louis Vuitton, and my proposal for this first phase of the project was accepted. My first consulting project for the company began in early summer 1976.

To help the client understand the situation in Japan as clearly as possible and to bridge the cultural gap, I decided to include many photographs in my report on the first phase of research.

To be able to work with people over long distances, with different ways of thinking and different linguistic, cultural, and sociological backgrounds, it is crucial to be able to share a common understanding.

Barriers to foreign investment

The second phase of the project was to find out how the European brands that had already entered the Japanese market, such as Gucci, Hermès, and Loewe, were marketed in Japan. This research would be informative and beneficial not only for Louis Vuitton but also for an industry outsider like myself. In other words, I learned at the same time I conducted the research.

For the third phase, I used my experience of almost ten years as a business consultant to determine what distribution channel the company needed. In the mid-1970s in Japan, when trade deregulation took place, I had mainly provided consultation services to joint ventures between Japanese and American companies.

Despite the gradual deregulation, foreign investment in Japanese companies was then limited to less than 50 percent in certain industries. Liberalization of capital eventually happened in the retail industry, but not more than ten stores could be operated. Most Japanese and foreign businesspeople assumed that with foreign capital alone, a bit of progress in legal liberalization wasn't enough to break into the Japanese market. Even securing qualified personnel was very difficult. This was the situation that foreign companies confronted when trying to break into Japan thirty years ago.

Most probably, Louis Vuitton expected to adopt one of the pre-existing distribution policies of European brands. Gucci had signed a contract with a specialty retailer, Hermès used a department store chain as its agent, and Loewe had established a joint venture with a wholesaler and another department store chain.

Based on my experience as a consultant, however, I was convinced that a general joint venture, in which a foreign company links up with a Japanese company, wasn't the best solution. As a Japanese proverb says, "Same bed, different dreams."

Problems with joint ventures

In most of these joint ventures, a foreign company introduced a new technology while its Japanese partner company manufactured and marketed the products. Even if the joint venture takes off, though, problems eventually develop between the two parties.

The foreign company believes the joint venture should be successful thanks to its technology. They reason: "Manufacturing and marketing are fairly straightforward, and we could have become successful by ourselves."

On the other hand, the Japanese company begins to have its own doubts: "We were told that their technology was extraordinary, but it turned out to be rather ordinary. We probably shouldn't have given them half of the capital and our expensive loyalty."

The relationship deteriorates further.

If the venture doesn't take off, or stumbles, while the

Japanese company blames the technology, the foreign company blames the ability of the executive officers on loan from the Japanese company. They begin to blame each other, and the relationship eventually collapses.

Evidence of this dynamic led me to believe that these problems occurred because the initial joint venture was a compromise, undertaken by both parties with too much optimism. The Japanese company assumed that they could save on the cost of technology development, while the foreign company assumed that they could cultivate the market quickly by leaving the manufacturing and marketing to the Japanese company.

I had seen many cases where joint ventures that were initially successful eventually collapsed. Hermès and Gucci distributed their products in cooperation with Japanese companies, but I was after a different distribution method.

While Louis Vuitton's name was quite well known at the time, it was still a small family business with only two stores under direct management, in Paris and Nice (today, 25 years later, there are more than 300 stores). In the American market, Saks Fifth Avenue controlled everything from manufacturing to selling under a license agreement.

Although the company could export some products,

it didn't have the staff to handle overseas business, or the funds to manage the business outside the country. It lacked the financial power and the human resources required to break into the distant Japanese market.

So I had to devise a completely new business model, one that wasn't a joint venture and also didn't require human resources or capital investment. That was the real beginning of my task as consultant, and I remained optimistic despite the obvious difficulties.

Two contracts

I imagined that Louis Vuitton would remain loyal to its brand policy and philosophy, even if it had to compromise slightly in the distribution area. While for Japanese companies, including trading companies, department stores, and retailers, Louis Vuitton was probably regarded as just one of many products they handled, but for Louis Vuitton, its brand was unique and irreplaceable. In my opinion, outsiders could not maintain the brand's value and history, established over many years.

I spoke with André Sacau, a consultant for Louis Vuitton in Paris who later became general manager of Louis Vuitton France, and we eventually devised a new system for procuring most of the operating funds locally in Japan, which would require very little investment from Louis Vuitton, while ensuring that distribution of the products remained under the company's strict control.

This system was based on two contracts:

1. A distribution contract
2. A management service contract

The distribution contract was to be agreed on between retailers (department stores) and Louis Vuitton Paris. Given that most of the department stores had branch offices in Paris, we requested that they pick up the products directly from the Louis Vuitton warehouse. This ensured that the business transaction was completed for Louis Vuitton by the time the products were shipped out of the warehouse. The department stores then shipped the products from Paris to Japan.

The management service contract was signed between the Japanese branch of Louis Vuitton and its business partners, especially the department stores. Under this contract, Louis Vuitton's Japanese branch would conduct all operations necessary for maintaining the brand image, protecting the trademark, undertaking quality control, advertising, and publicity. In return, it would charge franchise and management service fees to the department stores. These fees would then be used as the financial resource for the Japanese branch.

With both contracts, Louis Vuitton could conduct its international business as it did in France. This constituted a great advantage for Louis Vuitton France, which didn't have experience in international business or knowledge of export procedures. In addition, without such a contract, the newly established Japanese branch would not have been able to import the products, or carry out the customs clearance, or the warehousing and delivery to retail stores.

This was how Louis Vuitton successfully built a distribution system in Japan using little financial and human resources of its own. With this system, Vuitton didn't have to worry about logistics, including the delivery of products. At the time, it was probably our only option, but it was a completely new business model back then, and in the Japanese market it was considered beyond the Japanese common sense. It seems that under pressure, the human mind comes up with new ideas that often break the old barriers.

Controlling the entire process from production to distribution
Here is a list of the items that were included in the actual contract with the department stores:

1. The department store will set up a Louis Vuitton boutique in an agreed location within the department store, at the department store's expense.

2. The department store's employees will provide full sales services.

3. Only Louis Vuitton–specified supplies, such as wrapping paper, will be used.

4. The department store will cooperate to prevent price collapsing.

5. The sales staff will wear a uniform specified by Louis Vuitton.

6. Louis Vuitton will control advertisement, and the cost will be split between Louis Vuitton and the department store.

7. Louis Vuitton must approve any other advertisements in advance, including those paid for by the department store.

8. Louis Vuitton products will not be sold at events outside the store, or through the direct sales system known as *gaisho* (direct sales made by visiting the residences of important customers—such business could account for 20 to 35 percent of total department store sales in Japan).

9. The minimum order quantity specified in the contract will equal the maximum quantity, and Louis

Vuitton will not obliged to supply products exceeding that quantity.

Everything from store furnishings and staff uniforms to wrapping paper was to be determined by Vuitton. Although the sales staff was employed by the department stores, Louis Vuitton provided training for them in Paris and Japan. In addition, Louis Vuitton fully controlled the brand image through advertisements and publications.

Any advertisement proposals by department stores were declined, even if they covered all costs, because it was impossible to communicate a unified brand image without strict guidelines. I will come back to this in greater detail in Chapter 4 (*Building credibility*).

Our regulations were so specific that Louis Vuitton's products were excluded from the department store's members-only discounts and gift catalogues. In this way we were able to successfully establish a system whereby the brand's image and policy were completely maintained even without Louis Vuitton employees working in the stores.

Controlling everything from production to retail sales enabled us to run the business as if it were independently operated. We were particular about every detail because we wanted to accurately communicate not only the name of Louis Vuitton but the brand's values, which are its history and tradition.

Some say that the success of a brand is measured by name recognition, but I disagree. A brand is established only when the public fully understands its value. To achieve this understanding, the strategies for store operation, PR/advertisements and services, as well as the business model are all crucial.

To run a brand business successfully, you need to create a system with which you can control the entire process directly, from production to retail.

Not relying on the licensing

In the 1980s, the manufacture of imported brands through licensing boomed. Pierre Cardin became one of the most successful brands to market licensed products.

As a luxury brand, Louis Vuitton could have been tempted to make a profit through licensing in Japan, as they had a license agreement with Saks Fifth Avenue in the U.S., at that time.

I was convinced, however, that licensing, which didn't allow full quality control of products from manufacturing to retailing would not be fruitful. It might bring short-term profits, but in the long run, the brand image—or its credibility—could be at risk as a result of a lack of image and quality control.

The Louis Vuitton family agreed with this point of view. They treasured the brand and were very cautious about letting others use the name.

In essence, they didn't want to sell the brand name piece by piece. It was for this reason that the Louis Vuitton family agreed to "conclude a contract that fully supports the brand's intentions, even if it takes time." In addition, they were extremely patient during the negotiations with the department stores.

In truth, the contract was definitely to Louis Vuitton's advantage, so it wasn't always easy to get the department stores to sign it. It was to be the first time that a Japanese department store would agree to such a detailed contract with a supplier.

In the Japanese market, department stores had overwhelming power, and suppliers were happy to have their products displayed in the stores. It was unthinkable for suppliers to propose the terms and conditions in a written contract.

I later discovered that my ignorance of the business practices of the department stores probably worked to our advantage.

Negotiating with the department stores

I needed to devise a method so that the department stores would sign a contract that was beneficial to Louis Vuitton, so I set up a meeting with Vuitton's new General Manager, Yves Rogougneu, when he visited Japan in May 1977.

I also met with each department store, including Takashimaya, Seibu, and Sann Freres. I recognized then that Louis Vuitton could not get its way in these negotiations on a one-on-one basis, considering the size of the companies. Nevertheless, I thought most of the department stores valued Louis Vuitton as a brand with good potential and seemed keen to introduce Louis Vuitton products.

They obviously had very high expectations for the brand's future. When I outlined the contract to them, however, they were very reluctant. They replied: "We have never heard of such a contract. It is very unlikely that we will sign it."

So we came up with a new strategy. At the time, the team of Sann Freres and Mitsui Co. were the only legitimate Louis Vuitton dealers, and I had hoped that they would agree to the contract, although it was somewhat one-sided, in order to maintain their relationship with Louis Vuitton. Another tactic was to deal with at least two department stores that were different from each other. The more different they were, the better it was for us. We decided to focus our negotiations on Takashimaya and Seibu, who were most keen to negotiate a contract with us.

Conclusion of the consulting contract

Yves Rogougneu had wanted to end the relationships with Sann Freres and Mitsui Co. Our new business model directly connected the brand with retailers, so there was no further need for an import company (Mitsui Co.) and the wholesaler (Sann Freres).

Sann Freres, however, had been the first Japanese company to do business with Louis Vuitton, and I didn't want Louis Vuitton to be labeled as just another foreign company, with no sense of *giri* (obligation) or *ninjo* (humanity). As a consultant in charge of negotiations in Japan, and as a Japanese person, I wanted to avoid such a situation.

I persuaded Yves Rogougneu by saying, "Let's keep our business with them to show department stores that we have other business options. If the team of Sann Freres and Mitsui Co. accept our proposed contract and agree to give up the normal trading company and wholesaler margins, they can co-exist with department stores."

My proposal was based on the assumption that these department stores wouldn't want Sann Freres and Mitsui Co. to become the exclusive agents for Louis Vuitton, and would end up needing to procure the products through them.

With Louis Vuitton's popularity growing, our strategy triumphed. Six months later, over a three-day period, December 8 through 10, 1977, we concluded our contracts with the three companies.

The signing was a moving moment for me because it marked the conclusion of my consulting project, which had lasted for a year and a half. At this point, a new manager for the Japanese branch, to be appointed by Louis Vuitton, was slated to take over my job.

The idea was to open five sales points by March of the following year.

Two weeks before the press conference
But my job did not end then, after all.

At the time, I was also working for a Peat Marwick subsidiary called ECI, an executive search agency. One of my responsibilities was to find a suitable candidate for Louis Vuitton's Japanese branch manager. Consequently, I was conducting the executive search and the contract negotiations simultaneously.

At the end of 1977, Louis Vuitton's head office told me to stop looking. They had found a candidate in Paris—one of their relatives, a young man who had business experience in Japan and could also speak Japanese—and had decided to offer him the job.

By the new year, the preparation for the opening of the five new Japanese boutiques was proceeding smoothly. To mark the official opening of business, I was invited to Paris, along with representatives of Takashimaya, Seibu Department Stores, Sann Freres, and Mitsui Co., for a luncheon party with top executives from Louis Vuitton at the Restaurant Lasserre.

The day before the luncheon party, Henri Racamier, then a board member of Louis Vuitton, took me aside and said, "The candidate for the Japanese branch manager has business experience in Japan, but he has only worked for a bank. I don't think he has any experience with department stores or the distribution industry. We also cannot evaluate his Japanese-speaking abilities. Could you ask our Japanese guests to talk to him at the luncheon tomorrow and see if they think he is capable of running the business as branch manager in Japan?"

I explained the situation to the Japanese representatives and asked them to please evaluate the candidate. Following the luncheon, their unanimous feeling was that he did not appear capable enough to fill the role of branch manager. I conveyed their opinion to Henry Racamier, and the next morning he said to me, "We have had a family discussion, and we have decided not to appoint our candidate to the post. Furthermore, Mr. Hata, we would like you to become the acting branch manager for the time being. As you know, we will be having a press conference for the store openings in two weeks...."

I had no idea then that "for the time being" would turn out to be twenty five years, from then until today.

As a consultant, I had assessed the situation and proposed what I thought was the best possible system, one that was simple and efficient. Now I had been chosen to carry out my own plan. As *e-goso* (a "hard headed" man in Tosa dialect) and having just turned 40, I was determined to make my business model successful. 40-year-old men are supposed to be decisive, and at 40, I became the acting branch manager of Louis Vuitton in Japan.

When I graduated from university, I traveled to the United States to educate myself further and to pursue my dreams. When I graduated from business school, I turned down job offers from IBM and Esso to take a position at an accounting firm, so as to have future career flexibility. After acquiring experience in account auditing, I moved on to a consulting position.

After all these changes, at 40, I accepted the position of Japanese branch manager on a part-time basis for Louis Vuitton, but I didn't know that I would settle down in that position for good.

Sticking to our own policies

The operating agreement was officially signed through ECI K.K., and the branch office, which later became Louis Vuitton Japan K.K., began operating with one full-time female employee, two part-time consultants, and myself. It was a hectic beginning, with five stores opening at the same time, soon to be followed by a sixth one in Osaka Takashimaya, in September of that year.

Four years after the establishment of the branch office, in 1981, we converted it into a corporation and opened a freestanding store, the first one on Namiki Avenue in the Ginza district.

At that time, we decided to change the contracts to enable Louis Vuitton Japan to import products directly from Louis Vuitton France and distribute them to stores nationwide. We consolidated the distribution contract and management service contract into one, and shifted to an independent operating system whereby Louis

Vuitton Japan owned the inventory, maintained at Louis Vuitton shops within department stores.

The following year, after renewing all our contracts with the first six stores, we unified the contracts for all the stores and introduced a standardized system by which Louis Vuitton Japan has leasing contracts for staff and store space with its domestic business partners.

This model is completely different from wholesale. We operate our own business according to our basic policies, using store space and staff on lease. As a result of these actions, the business model we had built functioned to perfection and provided the foundation for Louis Vuitton's current success.

Marketing Louis Vuitton's tradition and history
Incorporating the brand's spirit into store design

Expression of the Louis Vuitton spirit

Louis Vuitton Japan's job is to sell products, not to manufacture them. Therefore, the stores play the most important role.

In 1976, when I first visited Louis Vuitton's main store on Avenue Marceau, it occupied the first and second floors, about 5,000 square feet, of a historic building. Many famous items from the brand's origins were displayed alongside the new merchandise.

When you stepped into the store, you could feel the history and tradition of Louis Vuitton. I had never seen a store like this in Japan. The common practice at the time in most luxury-brand shops in Japanese department stores was to display their merchandise only on showcases placed on the floor. A few of them had display shelves on the wall as well.

After my visit to the Louis Vuitton store in Paris, I became convinced that we needed to communicate the history, tradition, unique technology, and aesthetic of Louis Vuitton for the consumers to understand the brand's real value.

I also believed that the stores, where we had direct contact with customers, were the best vehicle to achieve this, especially given that advertising in Japan was too expensive for Louis Vuitton at the time. Failing to accurately conveying the tradition and history behind the products would be like "making a Buddha without the spirit," as a Japanese proverb says, and we wouldn't be able to expect the consumers to understand the "dream"—the real value—of the brand.

At the opening of the five boutiques in 1978, we displayed a large LV logo, as well as antique trunks by the entrance, to attract customers' attention immediately. A portrait of the founder, Louis Vuitton, was also displayed.

Although each shop occupied only a small space (approximately 700 to 1,000 square feet) in a department store, we made sure that they all stocked every size of the hard trunks—the symbol of Louis Vuitton's craftsmanship. We wanted the customers to feel the brand's essence the moment they entered the store, without the need for words. The size of our shops has increased dramatically to about 4,000 to 5,000 square feet in department stores, and 6,000 to 7,300 square feet in global stores (new concept stores for prêt-à-porter and shoes). But our general philosophy remains unchanged.

Opening five stores

Five stores—Takashimaya Tokyo (now Nihonbashi Takashimaya), Takashimaya Sanroser Akasaka, Seibu Shibuya, Seibu Pisa Osaka Royal, and Ann Royale Hankyu 17th Avenue—opened simultaneously on March 8, 1978.

This was the official beginning of Louis Vuitton in Japan. Up until then, Louis Vuitton had only had two stores—in Paris and Nice. With the opening of these five stores, the number more than tripled, and the fact that all the new stores were located outside France made it a big event. One more store opened in Osaka, a Takashimaya, in September of that year.

The first year was a very successful one. Despite a serious shortage of products, the total sales of the six stores amounted to 1,220 million yen ($5.8 million), for average monthly per-store sales of 23 million yen. This surprised the whole industry.

For a time, demand continued to exceed supply. To resolve this, we decided to focus on supplying the existing stores with products rather than opening more stores. As production from the French factory increased, the total sales at the six stores doubled, reaching 2,460 million yen ($11 million) in 1980. Each store achieved a two-fold sales increase in two years.

To be able to maintain our business contract, which was beneficial to Louis Vuitton, while keeping the department stores happy, we were determined to maintain the increase in sales in the existing stores. This promise has not been broken in twenty five years. The average monthly sales per store reached about 260 million yen in 2002, more than a 10-fold increase from the first year, while the total number of stores increased from 6 to 44.

Dreaming of a "brand street"

In 1981, Sogo Department Store planned to build a shopping complex called Sundarian in the Hokkaido Newspaper Building on Namiki Avenue in Ginza 7th Street. We decided to open the first freestanding store to be managed directly by Louis Vuitton Japan the building's ground floor.

This was a bold decision to make. Although Namiki had a unique atmosphere with long-established stores lining the street, there was only one shop—Sun Motoyama—that sold imported products.

Japan didn't have a "brand street," so-called because of a high concentration of luxury-brand shops, comparable to Avenue Montaigne or Rue du Faubourg Saint Honoré in Paris, Monte Napoleone in Milan, or Fifth Avenue in New York.

We pinned our hopes on opening a first-class shop in Namiki that would match the high-quality stores of Europe. We advertised for sales staff in July and hired six female staff members, including a store manager. We also prepared uniforms with the original design.

On September 9, 1981, we celebrated the opening of our first freestanding and directly managed store. Although we have opened other stores under our direct management since, our Ginza Namiki store was the first one in which we applied our current business model. It was also the first one to operate with our own staff instead of department store employees.

Reassessing the boutiques in department stores
By the end of the 1980s, as the number of stores exceeded 20, we began to reassess our shops in department stores. They had become too small to adequately handle the type and number of customers, as well as the amount of transactions.

We thus decided to move all Louis Vuitton shops located on the second floor and above, to the ground floor, the main floor of the department stores. Now "enclosed" luxury-brand shops on the ground floor of a department store are common, but at the time, the idea was greeted with surprise at the time. The department stores objected strongly to the plan. The ground floor was considered to be "the face" of a department store. Placing an enclosed brand shop on this important floor was unprecedented and unthinkable to them. I was determined to carry out the plan, however, even if it took five or ten years.

Louis Vuitton was becoming very popular with a wide range of customers beyond the "choice goods" floor. This made the ground floor, with its high traffic, very attractive for us. I also thought that we could create a shop on the main floor with an atmosphere similar to a freestanding store.

I began negotiating with department stores, confident that Louis Vuitton stores on the main floor would create a positive image for department stores and that Louis Vuitton customers would also generate sales in other areas. I discussed a projected sales increase in certain periods, guaranteed profits, and was even prepared to lose the contract.

Eventually, the Takashimaya stores in Tokyo and Kyoto agreed to relocate our shops from the second floor to the ground floor. The project to move all Louis Vuitton shops to the ground floor took more than ten years to accomplish and was finally completed only in 1990. The result has been a substantial increase in sales, and the department stores all seem satisfied.

Along with these relocations, we embarked on a reorganization plan in the mid-1990s, at the time of the collapse of Japan's "bubble economy." The plan was to operate the Louis Vuitton shops in department stores with our own staff instead of the department store's employees.

We began by assigning store managers and, after that, the assistant managers. With this reorganization, we have dramatically increased the number of employees of Louis Vuitton Japan. As of October 2003, we have 1,870 employees, with more than 1,000 of them having been added in the past five years. Our human resources department, responsible for recruitment and staff training, has been busy beyond belief.

The creation of global stores
In 1997, with the appointment of Marc Jacobs as artistic director, Louis Vuitton announced the launch of two new collections: prêt-à-porter and shoes.

This represented an enormous change for the stores, and large-scale "global stores" were created that could accommodate the whole range of products.

In Paris, the store on Avenue Marceau, which had long been the main store, was closed and relocated on the Champs Élysées, becoming the first global store in 1998. This one, like all the ones that followed, offers the full range of Louis Vuitton products, including prêt-à-porter and shoe collections, as well as trunks, bags, and accessories.

Peter Marino, the world-famous American architect, designed the interior of the global stores in a style that exemplifies the modern and fashionable aspect of the Louis Vuitton brand. Following the Champs Élysées store, a second global store was opened on New Bond Street in London, and a third one in Osaka's Shinsai-bashi on August 29, 1998.

Expanding the Louis Vuitton world

For the opening in 1999 of Louis Vuitton Japan's second global store, in Nagoya, our own design team undertook the interior design based on Peter Marino's concept. We also decided then to conduct the first design competition in Japan for the whole building.

We wanted to differentiate the global store from the existing Matsuzakaya, Mitsukoshi, and Meitetsu department stores in Nagoya, to focus on the Global Store's uniqueness. This gave us the freedom to be original in the design of our first freestanding store in a new building, offering the full range of Louis Vuitton products.

I have always been interested in architecture. One of my brothers-in-law, Masayoshi Yendo, is an architect and a former president of the Japan Institute of Architects, and there are many architects among my friends. When my brother-in-law was president of the Japan Institute of Architects, he worked hard to improve the social status of architects in Japan. He would often invite me to dinner and golf, saying, "I want to hear your opinion as an American-educated consultant."

All of this contributed to my desire to have a Japanese architect design our Japanese store. I wanted a store well-suited to the climate and the cultural characteristics of Japan and representative of Japanese architecture.

Many architects from Japan and overseas participated in the design competition. From among these proposals, Jun Aoki won the competition with his highly original design incorporating Louis Vuitton's tradition.

In Mr. Aoki's words, the building has "fuzzy external walls, like air, mist, or mirage. The building itself is an oblong cube, resembling a transparent jewelery case placed in the middle of the city." The façade is made of a glass surface with a wall behind it, re-creating the *damier* motif of the Louis Vuitton trunks.

That same year, Mr. Aoki also won the Architectural Institute of Japan Award, one of the most prestigious architectural prizes in Japan, and he designed our third Japanese Global Store in Matsuya Ginza in Tokyo, which opened the following year, in 2000.

The Matsuya Ginza Store was designed with the same basic concept as the Nagoya Sakae store, but it focused on harmony with the cityscape of Ginza. Furnished with materials such as large glass panels man-ufactured by Saint-Gobain (established by Louis XIV in the 17th century), the store strikingly distinguished itself from the rest of the stores as the "Louis Vuitton World."

The Omotesando building and "brand street"
The Omotesando building was completed in September 2002. Mr. Aoki, who had designed the Nagoya Sakae and Matsuya Ginza stores, also won the design competition for this building. His concept was to "randomly stack

Louis Vuitton trunks." In each "trunk" or component, a unique space unfolds. By creating a three-dimensional space that is perceived vertically rather than horizontally, his design creates a sense of unlimited spaciousness and depth. Moving from one floor to another, one travels through the space created by the different "trunks." Customers shopping there feel as if they are on a small journey. This architectural conception rests on the pleasure of the senses.

The opening of Louis Vuitton's Omotesando store changed the appearance of the street. The avenue of Omotesando, lined with elm trees, is a gracious and fashionable shopping area. Several popular and casual stores stand side by side in the little alleys behind the main street. Omotesando has drawn attention from many people around the world.

In recent years, many brand boutiques have opened in Omotesando. I believe that the Louis Vuitton Omotesando building added a breath of fresh air to the Omotesando area. It also enabled Louis Vuitton to communicate its view of the world to a wider audience and to further solidify the brand's image and existence.

I feel that the new Omotesando, where brands, fashion, and architecture are in unison, is the equal of the brand streets of Europe—the very image I dreamed of when we opened the first freestanding store on Namiki Avenue.

It can be said that the Lous Vuitton Omotesando building represents what we have achieved as a result of our recent architectural experience.

Focusing on architecture

Since the construction of the Nagoya Sakae store, Louis Vuitton has created a number of stores with this new approach. The Italian architects Philip Berthelemy and Silvia Grio designed our store in Kobe, and Kumiko Inui of Japan designed our Kochi store.

Little by little, the development of our stores in Japan has allowed us to collaborate with world leaders of modern architecture, giving way to a new relationship between architecture and fashion, attracting a great deal of attention in the world of architecture.

Consequently, in April 2003, we organized the exhibition "Louis Vuitton's Architecture." At the exhibition's symposium, the architects who have worked with Louis Vuitton talked enthusiastically about design specifics and the problems they experienced in the selection of materials. Essays written by the architects were compiled in a commemorative book, *Logique/Visuelle: The Architecture of Louis Vuitton*, under the

Nagoya Sakae (1999), the first independent freestanding
Louis Vuitton store in Japan.

editorial supervision of Mohsen Mostafavi, chair of the Architectural Association School of Architecture in London.

As Mr. Mostafavi states in the book, Louis Vuitton's strict policy to "build a life-size model of a part of the projected store on the actual site to see the impact on the environment before beginning construction" is different from common construction methods. This policy exemplifies the Louis Vuitton spirit, which can also be seen in the design and manufacturing process of our products.

The Roppongi store (2002) has a stone stairway with images projected by optical fibers built into the ceiling.

The great importance attached to the materials used is the spirit of Louis Vuitton. For me, a brand is part of the culture. Since opening our first shop in Japan, we have designed stores based on consistent and original concepts. It would give me great satisfaction to see that our store design in Japan has contributed to modern architecture.

The Roppongi Hills store
The Roppongi Hills store opened in September 2003. This is a global store in a completely new style, and the

only one in the world like it. We embarked on this project with the intention of utilizing the characteristics of Roppongi and creating a store with no equivalent elsewhere. To do this, we left aside Peter Marino's concepts for the interior design of global stores and undertook something completely original.

From the outside, the long translucent façade gives the impression of shimmering heat waves. Inside the building, metal curtains (the "skin") are used in place of inner walls to maintain the openness of the space. The staff uniforms were also completely changed. Business hours vary depending on the day of the week. The store stays open until 11 p.m. on Fridays, Saturdays, and Sundays so that visitors can enjoy entertainment in the form of shopping in Roppongi. Among several new concepts, my favorite is the "bag bar," where customers can sit down on a barstool and choose a bag over the counter. The bags are displayed on the wall just like bottles of drink.

The opening of the Roppongi Hills store was covered by a wide variety of media. The *Financial Times* of London printed an article with a photograph of the store on the first architecture page of its arts section—not the business section. With this, I felt we had successfully achieved a "fusion of fashion and art."

Surprises and novelty

Our stores continue to evolve, always incorporating new elements. Not unlike our slogan: "Louis Vuitton always provides surprises and novelty."

These big projects would have been impossible without the support and cooperation of the management and architectural teams in Paris. Louis Vuitton Japan is responsible for the sales and distribution of French-made products. "Surprises and novelty" corresponds not only to the products manufactured in France but to all the new stores created by Louis Vuitton Japan.

Our pricing policy
Honesty: the key to a successful business

The pricing process

Louis Vuitton Japan reviews its pricing once a year according to the fluctuations of the exchange rate between the Japanese yen and the French franc (now Euro) and makes adjustments as required.

This process has been carried out regularly for the past 25 years.

Before outlining the review process, I will explain Louis Vuitton France's fundamental retail pricing policy.

Louis Vuitton has existed for 150 years. It began as a made-to-order business, making one trunk at a time. The cost of raw materials plus labor costs were multiplied by a fixed rate. The price created by this calculation was the sale price charged to customers.

Since those days, our product line has greatly expanded and is now sold around the world, making the pricing process more complicated. The basic policy, however, has been maintained. We set our prices by multiplying actual costs by a fixed rate (gross margin rate), and we try to apply the same rate to all products. This is a unique approach.

The key to competitiveness

Our pricing method may appear anachronistic compared with modern marketing theories, which indicate that prices are set by taking into account such factors as competition, market conditions, consumption trends, and inventory status.

Louis Vuitton follows a different method. Our pricing process, which multiplies the prime cost by a fixed rate, is the best system to check the production costs for a luxury-brand business like ours.

Let us compare an estimated retail price achieved by multiplying the prime cost by a fixed rate, with other products in the market. If Louis Vuitton's price is higher, even with the quality and value for customers taken into consideration, it means that the production cost is too high.

We then conduct a thorough study to find a way to reduce the production costs without sacrificing quality. If we are unable to reduce the cost, we will not manufacture and market the product anymore, and so avoid the mistake of entering an unsuitable product area as well as lowering our overall profitability.

Louis Vuitton does not sell products at unprofitable prices simply to adapt to the market, nor does it reduce its prices because of excess inventory. I have no doubt that Louis Vuitton's adherence to this pricing policy has enabled us to achieve high competitiveness and reach the top position.

I respect Louis Vuitton's abilities in product planning, but what I admire most is its consistent attempt to reduce manufacturing costs without sacrificing quality, and the excellent result this achieves.

Products that last a long time

Of course, our pricing philosophy cannot apply to all industries. For example, it wouldn't work at all in an industry in which technology changes rapidly and new products are constantly being introduced. In the high-tech world, a technical innovation can slash the price of a chip by half, and a price reduction through mass production can increase competitiveness.

Our pricing process works well for us because Louis Vuitton is a luxury business—where craftsmanship, not mass production, is valued. Although compact discs have replaced phonograph records and DVDs have replaced videotapes, trunks have remained and will remain trunks. In addition, as opposed to electrical appliances, for example, the prices of which go down when newer products with the latest functions appear, Louis Vuitton's products acquire value over time. The longer you use them, the more attached you become to them. They also acquire a distinctive character, and older or used items are often more valuable than brand-new ones.

Though expensive, Louis Vuitton's trunks are sturdy and hardy. They can be used for many years and are compatible with the old Japanese way of thinking— to value goods by taking care of them well, so that they may be used for a long time—and are thus always environmentally friendly.

Our pricing policy

Louis Vuitton Japan's pricing policy was the industry's first pricing policy interlocked with the currency's exchange rate. Before joining Louis Vuitton, I had studied and worked in the United States for six years. Upon returning to Japan, I had been surprised to find that imported goods, especially European products, were extremely expensive.

Although products from Europe were relatively expensive in the United States, the price differential wasn't as large. Even before joining Louis Vuitton, I had felt as a consumer, that the price differential for imported goods between Japan and their country of origin was excessive.

At the time, there were many government restrictions in Japan on foreign investments by corporations, as well as on the amount of foreign currency that could be taken out of Japan by individuals. Even the spending of foreign currency by trading companies was limited to the dollars they had earned. Under such circumstances, importing foreign goods was considered extravagant. It was not surprising, then, that imported products were so expensive.

These were the factors that had led Japanese tourists to form long lines at the Louis Vuitton shop in Paris, and parallel importers to pretend to be tourists buying in bulk.

Louis Vuitton bags imported into Japan then cost three to five times as much as in Paris. I had the feeling that international trade and foreign exchange would gradually be liberated and that a new era, with a stronger yen, would come. Having done business in the United States and looked at Japan from the outside, I could anticipate this trend.

Once the project to implant Louis Vuitton stores had been established in Japan, I understood that pricing issues would be crucial. The extreme price gap between

Japanese and foreign markets was unacceptable and had to change, and I thought that an import business could succeed only without such huge price differentials. I started considering the possibility of lowering prices in Japan to narrow the gap.

When we opened our first Japanese store in 1978, prices in Japan were about 2.5 times as high as in Paris. Initially, I reduced the domestic prices to just double, then set a midterm target of reduction to 1.8 times and a long-term target of 1.4 times. The final goal was achieved a few years ago, and that ratio has been maintained.

Dishonest businesses don't last

In March 1979 the yen's appreciation against the French franc provided the perfect opportunity to shrink the price gap. I took advantage of the situation and created a plan to reduce the retail prices in Japan by 13 percent and informed our business partners, who immediately raised their concerns:

"You should avoid this at all costs. Brand products shouldn't be marked down. Customers value the products because they are high-priced."

"If a brand reduces prices, consumers think the brand is desperate to survive."

"You never know when the exchange rate will reverse. You should make a profit while you can, and prepare for the yen's depreciation."

Making a profit out of the exchange rate is against Louis Vuitton's spirit of honesty. An honest business should not take advantage of customers because they think expensive products are good. Dishonest businesses don't last.

In addition, a larger price gap would also increase the number of parallel imports. It was clear that a situation in which parallel imports were sold at unregulated prices everywhere would seriously obstruct the system we had just introduced. Despite our business partners' concerns, I decided to go ahead with the price reduction. I was determined not to let the consumers think we had reduced prices to survive, and I was sure we would succeed.

The response from customers

After the prices were reduced, we received a complaint from a customer who already owned one of our bags, claiming that it had been devalued.

She had bought the most expensive Louis Vuitton bag at that time, priced around 250,000 yen. We replied, "Price reduction doesn't mean devaluation of the products.

It means that the value of the yen has gone up. The price of imported goods decreases when the yen is stronger." But, the customer insisted, "Only Louis Vuitton lowered the prices. Other brands didn't."

I wanted to say it was because the middlemen were making all the profits, while Louis Vuitton was returning the profit margin to customers, but I couldn't. These days, more people travel abroad, and exchange rates are reported in the media every day. People can now easily understand Louis Vuitton's pioneering pricing policy.

The secret of successful price reductions

Unlike a conventional import business, Louis Vuitton Japan sells products under direct contract with retailers such as department stores. There are no trading companies or wholesalers involved. Direct sales simplify the distribution process, and cost savings are reflected in lower product prices.

Generally, the Japanese distribution channel is thought of as narrow, long, and complicated. The margins added in the middle push up the prices. There is, of course, a good reason for this system. Trading companies and wholesalers take their margins in compensation for the financial support they provide retailers who run their business with extremely small capital. They also take care of the import and currency-exchange process-es on the retailers' behalf.

On the other hand, retailers charge high margins in exchange for the risk of dead stock. The result is high prices for imported goods.

Our business model is based on product sales at directly managed stores; distribution costs for middle-men's margins are eliminated. This model also enables us to adjust prices as necessary. Another factor of our successful price reduction is efficient inventory control, in which demand always surpasses supply. The reduction of retail prices usually results in a smaller gross margin, because the appraisal value of the inventory remains unchanged.

Wholesalers and retailers, on the other hand, have many trading partners and a large amount of inventory. Therefore, they cannot reduce prices at their discretion. If they do so, with unsold stock, they end up selling at lower prices than initially planned, and their gross margin will shrink.

The same price for all customers
There are more important ways of using our energy, resources, and creativity than price wars. For example, improving products and service.

It is common for, initial prices to be set higher and store managers to decide the actual retail prices (the discount rate) at their discretion. They might offer lower prices to loyal customers while trying to sell at the set price to others. Such methods go against Louis Vuitton's pricing policy of offering the same prices to all customers.

Louis Vuitton is deliberately excluded from department stores' point-card schemes and bargain sales. In our 150-year history, Louis Vuitton has never conducted bargain sales or offered discounts.

Simplifying the operation by eliminating the variable factor of price fluctuation has added to the operational virtuous cycle.

It is important to concentrate on selling, instead of wasting energy on price negotiation. We need to focus on customers' needs through personal interaction. In this way, customers won't need to worry if they bought a product at the best possible price or whether they should have negotiated further. They also won't waste time waiting for the bargain season. Nevertheless, realizing this ideal requires strong merchandising capability.

Building credibility
Consistency in PR and advertisement

Promoting understanding of the brand, not the products

Louis Vuitton's corporate culture of "not to talk about ourselves" has been maintained since the establishment of the business. It is based on the belief that our products will carry our message, and embody honesty.

We had refrained from directly promoting or advertising our brand and our products. In the 1980s, when the bubble economy began, the so-called "brand boom" era arrived. The word "brand" grouped together various categories of products, including designer brands, character brands, and long-standing brands such as Louis Vuitton with a long tradition and history.

Although character brands were distinguishable from the others, consumers didn't know the difference between designer brands and long-standing brands. There is in fact a big difference between them. Designer brands depend on the designer's talent, while long-standing brands are sustained by craftsmanship, history, tradition, technology, philosophy, and aestheticism.

Wanting to stick to Louis Vuitton's policy of "not talking about ourselves," our challenge was to educate the public about the brand. Achieving this was a necessary step for the brand's internationalization.

Japan was where we first experimented with active brand promotion. I wanted to focus on the long-standing Louis Vuitton brand, not on its products.

When we opened the Japanese branch, Louis Vuitton's handbags were being mass-marketed by parallel importers in all major Japanese cities. My concern was that consumers would get the false idea that Louis Vuitton was just a handbag maker and a women-only brand.

Origins of the brand

To introduce Louis Vuitton as a long-standing brand, we organized the "Louis Vuitton Exhibition" at Nihonbashi Takashimaya in September 1978.

The purpose of this event was to introduce the roots of Louis Vuitton by exhibiting the brand's history from its creation. There were more than 10 articles on display, including a trunk for coach travel from the 18th century, a trunk that doubled as a bed (designed for an explorer), and an early *damier* canvas trunk. In addition, in a corner, the trunk production process was re-enacted by a craftsman, a process that has remained unchanged since its origins. The event provided an excellent opportunity for the public to understand the tradition and craftsmanship of Louis Vuitton.

Six years later, in 1984, a special exhibition called "Time Travel" was held. It juxtaposed Louis Vuitton's bags with illustrations on the history of travel. The exhibition started in Kobe and toured six other cities: Tokyo, Hakata, Sapporo, Nagoya, Yokohama, and Hiroshima.

Included in the show were a number of antique trunks and bags owned by the Vuitton family, as well as trunks for two-wheeled horse carriages. The exhibition was a sensation, and thanks to it, Louis Vuitton was able to solidify the message to the public that its origins lay in travel.

Targeting a male audience
We decided that we wanted to target a male audience to change Louis Vuitton's image as a "women-only" brand, and we chose to do this through interesting articles in magazines instead of typical advertisements. For the first project, we ran a series of interviews covering a double-page spread in a men's lifestyle magazine.

We selected famous Japanese men from various

fields who shared Louis Vuitton's values. For example, Shintaro Ishihara (originally a novelist and now the governor of Tokyo) talked about the appeal of a Louis Vuitton trunk from a user's viewpoint, while composer Yasushi Akutagawa spoke from his perspective as a traveling musician, about the differences and commonalities in sensitivity between the East and the West.

The interviews were not only about Louis Vuitton but also about the interviewees' work, lifestyle, and philosophy. Theater producer Keita Asari and filmmaker Kijuh Yoshida were also interviewed. Product advertisements were not included. Photos of the interviewees accompanied the interviews, and small photos of the Louis Vuitton products mentioned were shown discreetly in a corner of the double-page spread. The interviews were eventually collected in a booklet called "Louis Vuitton and I."

A second series was begun in 1985 with both male and female interviewees, including Yoko Yamamoto, the etching artist then based in Kyoto, and Danjuro Ichikawa, the Kabuki actor who had recently adopted that traditional stage name. This second series was collected in a booklet called "Louis Vuitton—Empathy with Originality."

Celebrating our 125th anniversary

In 1980 Louis Vuitton celebrated its 125th anniversary. A pictorial history of Louis Vuitton's 125 years was published in France. Included in this book was a collection of photos taken at the beginning of the 20th century by Jacques-Henri Lartigue, the great French "amateur photographer." Lartigue, who was still alive at the time, was also commissioned to take the photo for the title page of this book: a stack of Louis Vuitton trunks with the Eiffel Tower in the background.

In Japan a black-tie dinner party was held at Maxim's de Paris in the presence of Henry-Louis Vuitton, the fourth generation head of the family business, and his wife. It was a small gathering, with about 100 guests, but the media coverage successfully communicated Louis Vuitton's cultural impact. Such events were uncommon in Japan then. In fact, the public relations person in charge of the event worked so hard to make it a success that he fell ill the following day.

Advertising what we don't sell

No product advertising was done for two to three years after the opening of the Louis Vuitton Japan branch, with one exception: a newspaper advertisement stating "Louis Vuitton Does Not Make Neckties" published in

November 1978. And it was true, Louis Vuitton did not sell neckties in those days. A "representative of an Italian company," however, had visited Nihonbashi Takashimaya department store to sell "Louis Vuitton-endorsed neckties."

Fortunately, Takashimaya knew that Vuitton didn't make neckties and immediately informed us. If the "representative" had gone to a department store without a business relationship with Louis Vuitton, they might have believed him. And if some retailers had gone on to buy the ties, it would have damaged the brand's credibility.

Understanding the seriousness of the incident, we placed the ad warning against imitations of products—such as neckties, watches, and sweaters—that Louis Vuitton didn't produce.

It is very important for brands to take immediate action when such problems are identified. After this experience, we always took appropriate and swift action. This newspaper ad soon became a topic of conversation in the industry: "What a strange brand Louis Vuitton is; it doesn't advertise its own products but advertises those that it doesn't manufacture!" This was said because at that time, Louis Vuitton did not place any product ads in the media.

Louis Vuitton Japan's motto, "Be unique," was beginning to surface.

Communicating our tradition

In 1981 we carried out our first full-fledged product advertising campaign. It coincided with the establishment of Louis Vuitton Japan K.K.

The ad campaign, "Louis Vuitton—the Spirit of Travel," featured a series of magnificent photos by French photographer Jean Larivière taken all over the world and evoking luxurious trips, giving the irresistible desire to travel in such refined style. It was a true expression of Vuitton's history in the creation of travel-related products. In Japan, Louis Vuitton's manufacture of traveling trunks was not well known, and this series helped to increase people's association of Louis Vuitton with travel. The series continued for ten years.

Anecdotes from the Louis Vuitton legend

The history of Louis Vuitton is full of anecdotes. To show that the brand image was not just a simple façade but the result of a life full of experiences, we decided to produce a series of article-like magazine ads, particularly geared toward young people, centering on anecdotes of famous people involving Louis Vuitton bags.

One of them had to do with the Italian film director Luchino Visconti. Visconti had cast the 24-year-old Alain Delon as the lead in *Rocco and His Brothers*. When Delon first met Visconti, he saw his collection of Louis Vuitton trunks and remarked, "I can see that you are a director from a noble family. You even have special trunks with your initials, LV, printed all over."

Visconti, who always pursued excellence, loved Louis Vuitton for its quality and beauty and always took his own Monogram bag when he was filming. Louis Vuitton's Paris headquarters still has his customer card with his registration information, which includes his trunk key numbers. From that customer card, we found out that Visconti had in fact bought 42 Louis Vuitton products throughout his life. With his family's consent, we featured these items in an article. They included a large wardrobe trunk fitted with a hanger rack, a specially ordered director's chair, and a picnic set.

Visconti's last film, the posthumous *The Innocent* from 1976, was a story about early-20th-century Italian aristocrats. While directing the film, Visconti became obsessed with collecting Vuitton trunks manufactured in that era. He must have known that the Monogram pattern on these trunks was elaborately hand-painted back then, and his obsession with it had to do with the pride and aesthetic values he held as a descendant of an aristocratic and refined family. To him, these trunks were indispensable to illustrating the world he was seeking to describe.

Another anecdote used in the series was about the Louis Vuitton trunks used in Jean-Pierre Melville's 1970 film *The Red Circle*, starring Yves Montand. While the "Spirit of Travel" series had been a worldwide advertising campaign, these advertisements were unique to Japan and were based on a policy of "focusing on the understanding of the brand at an early stage of brand development, rather than on the products."

The reason for Japan-only ads

It is common to use universal advertising formats in every country to create a unified brand image. In France and other European countries, however, Louis Vuitton was already recognized as a brand with history and tradition. In the United States, the image of "luxury liners from the good old days" still prevailed. But in Japan, Vuitton's popularity had begun with its handbags and travel bags.

Consequently, I decided that specific PR and advertising activities were necessary to establish the proper brand image in Japan. After many efforts, I finally convinced Louis Vuitton France to agree to allocate 50 percent of their advertising budget to locally made ads in Japan.

To communicate a brand's value correctly, "consistency as a story" is more important than visually beautiful advertisements. Consistency helps to build up a brand's image and communicates to customers the brand's ideas and philosophy. One big difference between Japan and Western countries is that young Japanese women in pursuit of a fashionable lifestyle make up a substantial segment of the client population. Taiwan, Korea, Hong Kong, and China may follow suit, but this is nevertheless uncommon in Western countries.

Originally, luxury brands were only for people of a certain class. In the European social structure, possession of such products by others could even arouse suspicion of theft. In Japan, with its looser social structure, even young people can have brand-name products if they want to, and this is socially accepted. Some call it the democratization of brands. In my opinion, it has the positive effect of encouraging the free expression of personal values without the burden of convention.

In addition, Japan also has the traditional value of enjoying quality products for a long time. In other words, higher-priced quality products are considered to be a worthwhile possession and investment. This concept probably originated with the Japanese practice of conserving limited resources to enable a large number of people to live in such a small country. In turn, it has encouraged the acceptance of sturdy, long-lasting, and functional Louis Vuitton products in Japan.

Louis Vuitton's trunks, for example, are robust "boxes" that protect their contents. They are simple, water-resistant, rugged, and strong. Needless to say, elegant and fragile yet valuable brand products also exist.

Looking back over the past twenty-five years, I feel that the unique PR and advertising activities we undertook in the first ten years in Japan built the foundation for our success. Thanks to these, Louis Vuitton has grown steadily in Japan, and its Japanese market has become the biggest in the world.

The result of a worldwide survey on brand image conducted in the mid-1990s revealed that Japanese consumers knew the tradition and history of Louis Vuitton much better than their American counterparts.

This is remarkable, considering that Louis Vuitton had been better known in the United States since the era of the luxury liners, and that long before the Vuitton boom started in Japan, fashion models in New York traveled from one show to another carrying large Keepall bags, a Louis Vuitton classic.

"The most important thing for a long-standing brand is to communicate its tradition and history in a variety of ways" became our universal concept.

For a brand wishing to break into new markets, such as China, Louis Vuitton Japan's early PR and advertising experience could provide invaluable assistance.

Are brands status symbols?

Most criticism of brands is based on the claim that a brand is nothing but a status symbol, and people who buy brand products simply want status.

The Louis Vuitton logo is a case in point, as it is particularly prominent. Given that the Monogram series was the only product line until 1986, and with such a distinctive monogram pattern, the criticism was directed at us. To address this problem, we devised a communication strategy to focus on the particularities of the Monogram series.

First, we decided to emphasize the functionality of the material used for the Monogram series. The coated canvas is highly water-resistant, scratchproof, and easy to clean with simple wiping. The design goes well with a wide range of outfits regardless of age and sex.

Secondly, we explained the historical background of the Monogram pattern. The Monogram, which is one of the standard Louis Vuitton patterns, was originally devised to integrate the LV logo in the design so that the design itself could be trademarked.

The fact that the design combining the LV logo with star and flower motifs was devised more than 100 years ago is one of the brand's strengths; it proves that we didn't take advantage of the so-called brand boom (or brand-logo boom) to incorporate the logo into our products. The pattern, which may seem to be a status symbol, was actually designed to protect the trademark from forgery.

According to a survey conducted in September 2003, 44 percent of Japanese women between the ages of 15 and 59 own a Louis Vuitton bag. The Monogram may finally be breaking free of the "status symbol" stereotype.

Trust-building advertisements

In 1997 Louis Vuitton astonished the fashion world by appointing New York–based fashion designer Marc Jacobs as the artistic director for prêt-à-porter and shoes.

In Japan, while some people considered this unique combination very promising, others expressed their concern that Louis Vuitton would end up becoming a fashion brand after all.

The evolution of the canvas patterns reflects the company's fight
against counterfeiting.

To avoid this perception, we launched an advertising campaign that we later referred to as trust-building
ads. Three full-page advertisements were placed on the
Nihon Keizai Shimbun newspaper featuring hard
trunks. By showing Louis Vuitton's timeless value, we

aimed to send a message: "Although Louis Vuitton is fashionable, it will never be a fashion brand."

The ads emphasized Louis Vuitton's focus on service— the fact that service is part of our products. The ads had the following slogans:

1. Louis Vuitton is repairable
2. Robust promise
3. Even for initials

In the "Louis Vuitton is repairable" advertisement, we emphasized our repair service by showing a photograph in which all the parts used in a trunk were lined up side by side. We also promised a long life for Louis Vuitton products.

The "Robust promise" advertisement focused on the tradition that a unique key for each trunk is registered and given to a customer at the time of purchase, indicating a relationship of mutual trust. For customers who have more than one trunk, a unified key number for all trunks is provided and registered in a ledger. This key registration has existed since the business was established. The "Even for initials" ad featured our service for painting personalized initials, thus sending a message that we meet every customer's needs.

When I go to the south of France in the summer, I sometimes see Louis Vuitton bags that have been personalized like this, and I recognize that it is a practical way of recognizing one's luggage at a baggage pickup area, where Louis Vuitton bags can be easily mixed up with others.

This trilogy of ads won a number of prizes as well as great responses even from people who were not familiar with Louis Vuitton.

Maintaining the balance

A publicity campaign for prêt-à-porter and shoes created by Marc Jacobs was launched in 2000 around the world. One of the series, called "The Seven Sins," attracted a great deal of attention for its eccentric photographs.

We have also continued our efforts to create ads suited to situational and social changes in Japan, including trust-building ads meant to surmount the seeming contradiction between permanent values and the world of fashion. Success as a real brand now depends on our ability to overcome this paradox, combining "traditional values" with "keeping up with the times."

Mythologizing our service
Diversified customer service

The Japanese value good quality

Although Louis Vuitton had been devoted to the production of high-quality items with superior craftsmanship since the brand's establishment, paradoxically, quality has been further enhanced since we started doing business in Japan.

In the Japanese market, where even a slight imperfection is considered to be a defect, we faced many challenges dealing with defective products.

During the first 10 years, we have often found ourselves having to return products to Paris saying, "This level of quality is unacceptable in Japan." At first we had a very hard time being understood. If we returned a product because the fastener was attached the wrong way, they argued that we should sell it to a left-handed customer. If we complained that the stitches were not straight, they said it was because of the nature of hand stitching and that they could sell the products in Paris without a problem.

On one occasion we returned all the products, say-ing, "Please sell these in Paris." It was very hard to make them understand the problems.

It seems to me that the Japanese are the most demanding customers in the world, because they under-stand and value good quality in its most positive sense.

In those days, there were no fax machines or e-mails, so communication with Paris regarding such details was slow and painstaking. In an effort to get my point across about market and cultural differences, I found myself sending a large number of telexes to board members and stockholders (who at the time were all members of the Vuitton family). My long telexes, which were rolled up into a big roll of paper, were known in Paris as "the *makigami*" (ancient Japanese letters in rolled paper) from Japan.

Our determination eventually bore fruit: the quality control system in Paris was finally reformed.

Never fall short of customers' expectations

A brand should never fall short of customers' expecta-tions, because their high expectations are in fact the rea-son they come back. The more value customers find in products, the higher their expectations.

Louis Vuitton's reputation used to be that its products were "unbreakable"—not just "sturdy" but "unbreakable."

This is not a bad reputation, of course, but it would inevitably lead to complaints and a loss of credibility if anything went wrong, which would be hard to overcome. In fact, how could we have responded to such a complaint?

In order to transpose the myth to reality, we did two things. We improved our repair services, and we conveyed a new message: "Our products are very sturdy, but they may wear out after years of use. Our repair service will extend the life of the product."

There is no doubt that after many years of daily use, a fastener will wear out. We cannot offer unbreakable products, but our repair services can ensure continued use. Improved repair services is crucial to customer satisfaction.

If customers didn't initially expect anything, they wouldn't come back for repair. If they simply threw away broken products, there would be no need to improve repair services. It is because our clients expect a lot from our brand that the improvement of our repair services became another challenge for Louis Vuitton Japan.

The creation of the Repair Service Center

Shortly after opening our first store in Japan, we embarked on the establishment of our own repair system in Japan. We recruited skilled Japanese craftsmen and sent them to Paris for training. In addition, we had all necessary parts for product repair shipped from Paris.

For a time, it was very hard to order and sort the parts correctly because so many of them were small and they all had unusual French names. Nowadays when a new product launch is expected, we begin preparing its repair methods and a parts inventory at the developmental stage.

For us to repair a product means, for example, that the original stitches must be accurately traced. This entails removing the original stitches first, then putting a needle through each of the original needle holes. That is why the more novel a design is, the more caution is required during the development stage to take repair work into consideration.

About twenty years ago, we had only about 500 products, including a variety of colors and sizes. This number is very small compared with many fashion brands, which typically have around 5,000 items, with new products being added every season. Discontinued products may be modernized and revived. Fashion from the 1960s and 1970s may come back, for example, but every item needs to maintain a common basic element.

The scale of our repair services expanded along with our sales growth. In 1993 our first service center in the world was established. Today we have five dedicated repair centers in Japan—in Tokyo, Osaka, Nagoya, Fukuoka, and Kobe.

To attract customers, it could be more effective to set up a repair counter within a store. Then a customer would have to visit the store at least twice, to bring in and to pick up the product. We decided, however, to separate the repair centers from the stores so that everyone could concentrate fully on their job.

Service is part of quality

Louis Vuitton's business began originally as a *layetier-emballeur* (trunk maker) based on made-to-order production. This tradition is carried on today with our Special-Order Service.

Skilled craftsmen in Paris individually made special-order items. After launching the "Epi" collection in Japan, we received many orders for hard Monogram trunks, but made with the Epi material. In May 1993 we established a Special-Order Service section with one

"Louis Vuitton is repairable" was one of the newspaper ads we placed,
showing all the parts in a rigid trunk.

full-time employee, meant to consolidate all special orders received in Japan and communicate them to our colleagues in Paris. The section's only staff member handled about 100 orders in the first year alone.

In October 1993 the first Special-Order Exhibition was held in Tokyo and Kobe, intended to introduce our special-order service to a wider audience. Actual special order products were displayed, and Patrick Louis Vuitton, fifth-generation heir of Louis Vuitton, in charge of special orders, was present for customer consultation.

One of the orders received during the exhibition was for a Kimono case, a very Japanese creation. In fact, we have received many unique orders in Japan, such as a *nodate* (outdoor tea ceremony) tea set case originally made for a grand tea master, which has become a standard special-order item here.

Today we receive a wide variety of orders—ranging from Monogram items made with *damier* material to unique custom-made items. Following the launch of the shoe, watch, and jewelry lines, orders for large shoe cases, watchcases, and jewelry cases have increased.

The spirit of the trunks

Louis Vuitton's trunks, the brand's original product, are fitted with a special security lock (*boîtier*) designed by

Louis Vuitton himself. The lock system, patented in 1890, originally had five internal wings, but it now has six to accommodate the growing number of registrations.

For a customer who owns more than one trunk, key numbers can be unified so that one key unlocks all of them. Each key number is permanently registered in Louis Vuitton's customer file. The customer files have been kept with meticulous care since the brand's establishment, protecting the personal information of our customers. The customer's name, date of purchase, key number, and specification of the purchased product are recorded on each card.

Every time a customer purchases a trunk from a Louis Vuitton store anywhere in the world, his or her key number is communicated to a special division in Paris, and the lock bearing the same key number is made and then sent and fitted to the purchased trunk. If a customer loses their key, the key will be reissued and delivered after confirmation of ownership against the customer file.

According to the customer files, the first Japanese person registered was Shojiro Goto, a statesman who played an important role in the Meiji Restoration (in the year 1867). He was originally from Tosa, where Ryoma Sakamoto (a famous samurai who contributed to the end of the feudal era) was also from. The records say that he purchased a large trunk, 110 centimeters wide, on January 30, 1883. Goto left the port of Yokohama with Taisuke Itagaki (a famous politician at the time) on November 11, 1882, and landed in Marseilles after a sea voyage of about fifty days. During his stay in Paris, he visited the Louis Vuitton main store, which was then on the Rue Scribe.

To think of Goto visiting our store in Paris is emotional for me, as I am also originally from Tosa. Unfortunately, Shojiro Goto's trunk was stolen and has never been found. Louis Vuitton, however, keeps a replica of it today.

The establishment of a service committee

Although there are already many myths surrounding Louis Vuitton products, we decided to create a new myth in the field of service, and we chose "Mythologizing our service" as an internal key phrase for our employees in early 1997.

We set up a service committee with a delegate from each section to review our current services. Its members also discussed service provisions for the future and offered new ideas on customer service. We also began to circulate an employee newsletter containing letters of appreciation from customers and awards received from department stores. In order to review our in-store services as well as the store's facilities, we had external examiners carry out spot checks by pretending to be customers. Because only a limited number of employees were informed of the checks in advance, the results released the following year were a big surprise for most of the staff.

Sometimes our long-standing, loyal customers also help us to improve our services by giving us their honest opinions about our products. Although we should be aware of any shortcomings before our customers point them out, we value their opinions highly. It is important to know how to take their criticisms and to have a response for them.

In 1996 we established the Customer Information Service (CIS) as a division to deal with all inquiries from our customers. Its purpose was to enhance the communication channels between our customers and Louis Vuitton. Since many inquiries were being received at our stores by phone, the establishment of the centralized inquiry service center enabled the staff of our stores to concentrate on product sales. In addition to providing product information, the CIS also offered after-sale services for products purchased in Japan and overseas.

The number of calls increased every year, and more than 80 percent of the inquiries were related to our products, so in 2001 we set up a call center to specialize in telephone inquiries. All telephone inquiries, from available stock to reservations for new products, are now centrally handled by a toll-free system. As of September 2003, 40 operators attend to more than 550,000 calls a year.

Customer service unique to Japan

Our first customer-service scheme unique to Japan was catalogue sales. This system, which was later named Direct Order Service, began in April 1986 as the product catalogue section of the Ginza store (with two staff members).

The catalogues, which included all Louis Vuitton products, were produced in Paris. Along with catalogue sales, we also began to receive orders by phone. One of the factors that led to the creation of this new service was an incident that took place in 1985.

A mail-order company had started to sell Louis Vuitton products, procured by parallel imports, through a large-scale newspaper ad campaign leading some customers to believe that Louis Vuitton had begun a mail-order business. Mail order was then considered a second-class business in Japan and we were concerned that this would have a negative impact on our brand image.

In addition, the prices offered by the mail-order company were much higher than ours were, and we feared that it might eventually damage our credibility. Following our policy of taking immediate action against such signs of trouble, we placed a full-scale newspaper ad that said: "Beware of mail-order sales with monthly installments that have no relation with Louis Vuitton."

Soon after, Louis Vuitton began its own catalogue sales, to avoid the danger of further illegitimate mail-order businesses. Because at the time we had only seventeen stores in Japan, this service enabled customers all over Japan to purchase our products easily.

In 1992, due to the overwhelming number of incoming orders, we abolished manual order handling and introduced a computerized system. In response to customers' requests, we established full-scale nonstore operations and started accepting payment by credit card and COD. We also began new promotional activities, such as seasonal direct-advertising mailings, which are particularly useful for customers not living near a Louis Vuitton store or for those who wish to purchase products quickly.

As a result, our Direct Order Service has become our

48th store, complementing the 47 stores nationwide.

In October 2003 we began offering catalogue sales over the Internet. The development of Internet business, and catering to its needs, is now a major challenge for us.

Pursuing the "Never say no" service

To achieve the objectives of "Mythologizing our service," we faced the challenge of improving the quality of our customer service at each store to enhance customer satisfaction.

As the number of stores increased, unified customer-service standards became necessary. Yet, to strictly follow a customer-service manual cannot satisfy customers' requirements. Consequently, we decided to have an annual meeting with the personnel in charge of the Direct Order Service, Repair Service Center, Special Order Service, Call Center, and Quality Assurance departments. Each of the representatives then reports back to the staff in the stores on the current service activity.

Until recently, our Repair Services department's policy was to turn down repair requests in cases where the repair cost exceeded the product's retail price. Replacing the leather surface of a Monogram purse is one example. If one puts oneself in the customer's shoes, however, having a repair request turned down represents a lack of service. If, for example, a damaged bag is a precious memento from a loved one, restoration may be more important than cost. For this reason, a client's request cannot simply be turned down because of a certain policy. It is reasonable for a client who has a bag full of good travel memories to want to use it for many years, even with repairs.

Our staff discussed ways to make the most of the Japanese virtue of taking care of quality products so that they can be used for a long time, and we decided on a "Never say no" service policy, by which any repair request is considered positively.

Launching a concierge service

A new service debuted with the opening of the Omotesando Store in 2002 called Concierge Service.

A concierge originally meant a member of the staff of a hotel who can provide various services for the guests, including general information and sightseeing tour arrangements. The role of the concierge has now expanded to providing specialty advice and local information. Experienced concierges in European hotels have more knowledge and information than any guidebook can provide, and can easily cater to almost any request from a guest.

Louis Vuitton's concierges have extensive experience and knowledge about our products. They strive to cater to a wide variety of customer requests by being up to date on the latest information and expanding their networks. As the first person to greet a customer at the store, the concierge also plays the role of a hotel doorman. In addition, they try their best to greet known customers by name, and can recommend suitable items to customers shopping for a gift.

Apart from shopping-related services, Louis Vuitton concierges can also handle hotel and restaurant reservations, arrange for taxis and chauffeur-driven cars, and provide information on theaters and nearby shopping areas. Our concierges aim to provide even better service than hotel concierges do. This service has emerged from our desire to offer shopping as a kind of entertainment. It is in this spirit that we will continue to provide "never say no" service and aim to "mythologize our service." Each customer's satisfaction positively affects the brand's reputation, which in turn determines the brand's value. In my opinion, there is no end to what one can do to improve service.

Eliminating excuses not to buy
The challenge of new product development

Excuses to buy and not to buy

Louis Vuitton's production is controlled at its head-quarters in France. Louis Vuitton Japan does not directly participate in product development. But as a business responsible for the Japanese market that makes up more than a third of its worldwide sales, we offer strategic advice based on our market.

In her book *The Chrysanthemum and the Sword: Patterns of Japanese Culture*, Ruth Benedict, a cultural anthropologist, defines the "shame culture" of Japan. For my part, I think I have discovered what I would call the "excuse culture"—a kind of consumer psychology—by looking at the purchasing behavior of Louis Vuitton customers in Japan.

When it comes to Louis Vuitton products, Japanese customers seem to need an excuse to buy them or not to buy them.

Let us imagine a woman carrying a new Louis Vuitton bag. Her friend says to her, "You bought a new bag, didn't you?" The woman might reply, "Yes, I went to Paris last month and bought it on impulse." Her "excuse" is that she happened to be in Paris and saw the bag.

Behind the excuse may lie some guilt for buying another bag when she already has several. To a direct question such as, "How could you buy such an expensive thing?" she might say, "It's durable. Quality products are a better value in the end." In addition, she might throw a question back, "Don't you think so?"

On the other hand, an excuse not to buy might be because of a preference for leather bags, a dislike of distinguishable patterns, or its ubiquity in Japan. We can only guess at the truth. Even if we conducted a survey, we might never really know the consumers' reasons for buying or not buying. Although this knowledge would be very useful for product development, it probably falls more in the category of psychology, than in that of marketing.

Eliminating excuses not to buy
People who don't buy Louis Vuitton products have their own reasons (excuses). Some may say that they don't want to be the same as everyone else; others may say Louis Vuitton bags are practical but lack class. To counteract

some of these excuses, we have undertaken several measures.

For those customers who prefer leather we introduced the "Epi" line of leather bags; for those who dislike the Monogram we introduced plain materials; and for men we introduced the "Taiga" line. Such changes have also offered us the opportunity to review the functionality of existing products, such as durability and stain resistance.

In a magazine article by young novelist and musician Kenichi Yamakawa, he refers to a short story by Kenji Miyazawa, one of Japan's most read and beloved authors, "Leather Trunk." The main character of the story fails in his profession of architecture and runs away to Tokyo. He returns home after hearing that his mother is ill. Before returning home, he spends 20 of his total 30 yen—all he possesses—to buy a leather trunk. Since he has nothing to put in the trunk, he fills it with old architectural drawings. Back home, his father, a village chief, gives a wry grin when he sees the trunk and its contents.

The character is a reflection of the author himself, who had gone home to Hanamaki (Kenji's hometown, a small town in northern Japan) to see Toshi, his sister who was ill, with a trunk full of manuscripts of children's stories. Miyazawa is known for his moralistic poems, but this story reveals a rather unknown part of his personality, one of an elegant dandy taking care of his linen suit, far from the image he is known by of the poor man's passionate poet. Yamakawa concludes the article by saying, "If Kenji lived in Tokyo today, he would choose Louis Vuitton's Monogram trunk."

Our wish is that more men will recognize Louis Vuitton bags as products and enjoy them without prejudice. To achieve this, it will be important to discover men's reasons for not buying our products, and then do our best to eliminate them.

The launch of the Epi line
Forty percent of Japanese women between the ages of 15 and 59 reportedly have Louis Vuitton products today. A number of very successful products have contributed to the fact that so many Japanese women own Louis Vuitton products today.

The introduction of the Epi line in 1986 was a turning point. Yet when the French product development team first visited Japan with a sample before the launch and explained the new product's concept, the Japanese staff had a mixed response. We worried that the characteristics of Epi—bright colors such as green and red, and the use of leather—were very different from the

Monogram line and that it would not be in harmony with the traditional line. Although some of the young sales staff commented favorably, many of those who had been involved with Louis Vuitton for a long time expressed some resistance.

Despite these concerns, the new line gained immediate and huge popularity. The media featured the new products, and sales at the stores were excellent. In a short period of time, the Epi line became a big trend.

The success of the Epi line eliminated one of the excuses not to buy, by offering leather bags, while also freeing Louis Vuitton from the dominant image of the Monogram. In my opinion, the rapid growth of Louis Vuitton began when the brand overcame the pressure of the Monogram's tradition and great success.

Paradoxically, the introduction of Epi leather products provoked a renewed appreciation for the Monogram line's functionality and durability.

Introducing new products and acquiring new customers
There have been other successful items that have contributed to a widened customer base. When we launched the sporty "Saumur" bags in 1987, customers waited in long lines for the stores to open all over Japan. "Alma" became a big hit in 1993. Its design was based

on a bag Coco Chanel special-ordered in the 1920s. Even though the only advertising we did for it was in the form of direct mailing to our clients, some stores had a waiting list of one year.

In 1994 we launched Taiga, the first line designed for men. By targeting elite businessmen, the new line successfully acquired new Louis Vuitton fans. Although we had previously offered products for men, Taiga eliminated the excuse often heard from men unfamiliar with the brand that "Louis Vuitton has no products for men."

A history of innovation

The wooden-trunk artisan Louis Vuitton began his business in 1854 when he opened a travel bag store near the Opera in Paris. At the time, there were no other stores specializing in travel bags. Opening a specialty store was Louis Vuitton first challenge.

The French word *malletier* in the official company name, Louis Vuitton Malletier, means "trunk maker." Louis Vuitton used to make wooden boxes to contain dresses with crinoline flared-out skirts for the royal family and the aristocratic classes. The wooden boxes of the time were carried on horse-drawn carriages and had a rounded lid to repel the rain. To re-cover them, a varnished plain gray canvas, *gris trianon*, was used, lighter than leather and water-resistant. Later, Louis Vuitton, who had a modern and rational way of thinking in addition to extensive experience in craftsmanship, decided to adapt the trunks to new traveling methods such as trains and steamboats, and the lid was flattened to facilitate stacking.

With the advent of new modes of travel, Vuitton invented trunks that could be carried easily onto the cabins of ships or trains. These trunks, which could hold enough for a long journey, changed the concept of traveling and enjoyed great popularity.

With the increased success of his reputation as a trunk-maker, Louis Vuitton continued to develop new products in line with the newer travel methods: cars and airplanes. The source of product development at Louis Vuitton since the beginning has been its sensitivity to the times, and the technology needed to create new products according to changing needs. The founder's spirit and the idea of traveling are embodied in all Louis Vuitton products.

Collaborating with artists
When Louis Vuitton merged in 1987 with Moët Hennessy to form LVMH, product development entered a new phase. The next year, "Nomad," a high-quality men's bag made of natural cowhide, was introduced.

In addition, a collection of watches, scarves, and fountain and ballpoint pens made as the result of a collaboration with several artists was introduced.

This new line of products, "Journey of Creation," was launched simultaneously in Paris, New York, and Tokyo. Gae Aulenti, the Italian designer responsible for the conversion, the old Orsay train station in Paris into the Orsay Museum, was commissioned to design Vuitton's watches and pens. Five famous architects and artists—Arata Isozaki, James Rosenquist, Arman, Sandro Chia, and Sol LeWitt—were commissioned to design a collection of twenty-six scarves on the theme of "the Silk Road."

Although the series didn't achieve a big commercial profit, it successfully communicated Louis Vuitton's commitment to creativity and conveyed our ability to constantly explore new areas. This experience also allowed us to set the foundation for a policy of innovation and of collaboration with artists.

A new Monogram challenge

In 1996, in commemoration of the Monogram design's centennial, we asked contemporary designers to create a special edition of bags based on the Monogram canvas. Seven designers participated in this project: Azzedine

Alaïa, Isaac Mizrahi, Helmut Lang, Romeo Gigli, Vivienne Westwood, Sybilla, and Manolo Blahnik.

Each of them created highly personal, creative, and innovative designs that expertly fused the monogram material and superior craftsmanship. Their creations perfectly embodied Louis Vuitton's tradition and innovative spirit.

The emergence of Marc Jacobs

New York-based designer, Marc Jacobs was appointed as the brand's artistic director in 1997. Still in his thirties, the young designer was already drawing much attention around the world.

He created new product lines, including prêt-à-porter and shoes, that added a new dimension to the Louis Vuitton world built on tradition and craftsmanship.

For the 2001 Spring/Summer collection, Jacobs collaborated with avant-garde artist Stephen Sprouse on the design of Monogram bags painted with graffiti. This collaboration was inspired by a visit Jacobs made to actress Charlotte Gainsbourg in her apartment. There he saw a Louis Vuitton suitcase that she had inherited from her father, Serge Gainsbourg. It was painted black but with the Monogram showing through. Jacobs conceived then the idea of integrating Louis Vuitton's old tradition with modernity, by asking Sprouse to paint graffiti on the Monogram.

It was daring to radically change the appearance of the Monogram canvas, yet the company's insight and flexibility heralded a new era for Louis Vuitton. "Louis Vuitton's history is a gold mine of ideas for me," Jacobs said, "and applying ideas and designing accessories is very stimulating and great fun."

Collaborating with Takashi Murakami

The evolution of the Monogram accelerated when Marc Jacobs met contemporary Japanese artist Takashi Murakami in 2002. Jacobs had taken it as a challenge to work with the Monogram canvas, and he was looking for a contemporary artist to develop its potential.

He was attracted to Murakami's strong individuality and his childishly innocent but somewhat ironic style, and he invited him to Louis Vuitton's workshop. The fruit of this encounter is now history.

Murakami had majored in Japanese painting at the Fine Arts department of the Tokyo National University of Fine Arts and Music, and he was the first Japanese-style painter to acquire a doctorate degree. His work was, in fact, more highly valued abroad than in Japan. The new "Monogram Multi-Color" was printed in thirty-

Special edition bags (from left to right, bottom to top): Azzedine Alaïa, Manolo Blahnik, Helmut Lang, and Romeo Gigli.

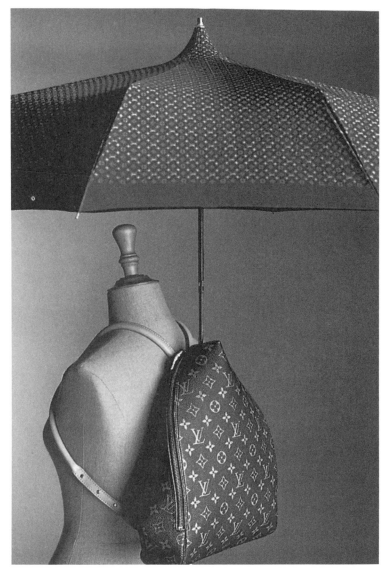

The centenary, in 1996, was a great opportunity to attract the public's
attention to Louis Vuitton's heritage, craftsmanship, and future-oriented
innovative spirit. A collaboration with seven gifted designers gave rise
to the creation of a limited edition of commemorative items.
Shown here, a model by Sybilla.

three colors. The "Eye Love Monogram" series, printed in sixty-two colors with ninety-three silk screens using advanced technology, was a true work of art.

As part of a large-scale special display to commemo-rate the product launch at the Omotesando store, a huge LV Panda created in collaboration with Murakami was placed at the main entrance. This special event also dou-bled as an art exhibition to mark the new era of Louis Vuitton.

A *fusion of art and practicality*

Through its collaborations with artists, Louis Vuitton has sought to integrate artistry into its products. Bags and art may appear unrelated, but it can probably be said that a taste for art increases when people become wealthier. In addition, products made for daily use, with the greatest craftsmanship, though unsuitable for mass production, can also be artistic. Pottery from Bizen (one of the six ancient kiln sites in Japan where pottery has been pro-duced for more than 1,000 years) is one such example of this.

Along with artistry, the practicality and function-ality of our products is essential. Finding a way to offer per-manent value while keeping up with trends is the key to success in the luxury-brand business. Creating highly artistic products at reasonable prices remains one of our challenges for the future.

An ever evolving brand
Entering new business sectors

The path to diversification

Starting with its entry into the Japanese market, Louis Vuitton, which had long been a family-owned business, began its transformation into an international company expanding into the world market. Simultaneous listings at the Paris and New York stock markets in 1984 facilitated the company's desire to explore ways to diversify. Louis Vuitton had begun his business as a trunk maker, and he had adhered to his specialty, refraining from business diversification.

When a brand becomes famous, it is tempting to increase sales by expanding product lines into unfamiliar fields. If the company doesn't have the technology and skill to do so, however, it ends up by selling products made by other companies under its own brand name.

For this reason, Louis Vuitton's management chose to diversify by acquiring established top brands rather than expand into unfamiliar fields. The first example of this stategy was the company's merger in 1985 with the prestigious champagne company Veuve Clicquot. (It should be added that the fact that one of Louis Vuitton's external board members then owned a champagne company might have encouraged this deal.) Although the two companies belonged to different industries, the merger was practical for both of them, as they shared the same set of values built on French history and tradition.

That same year, Louis Vuitton also acquired the international distributorship for Loewe, the famous Spanish brand of leather products, and established Loewe International.

The birth of LVMH

Two years later, in 1987, Louis Vuitton completed a merger with Moët Hennessy, establishing LVMH (Moët Hennessy–Louis Vuitton). Moët Hennessy's principal business was in cognac and champagne, a completely different field from that of Louis Vuitton. Even after the merger, the two businesses continued to operate independently.

The merger, however, enabled Louis Vuitton's mainly flow-based business and Moët Hennessy's mainly stock-based business to complement each other, resulting in a company with financially more stable and balanced growth opportunities.

In 1988, the following year, because Parfums Givenchy had become a subsidiary of Louis Vuitton through the merger with Veuve Cliquot, the company also acquired Givenchy Couture.

The appointment of Bernard Arnault as president of LVMH's management committee accelerated the acquisition of fashion brands into the group. The fashion brands previously owned by Mr. Arnault, through a holding company called Financière Agache (Christian Lacroix and Celine) also joined the group.

These acquisitions provided the basis for Louis Vuitton's financial growth as well as its operational effectiveness. In other words, the foundation for Louis Vuitton's advance into the fashion business had now been set.

The emergence of new management

In 1990, on Bernard Arnault's recommendation, Yves Carcelle was appointed President of Louis Vuitton France.

Carcelle was a graduate of the École Polytechnique, the same elite French school that Arnault had attended. Although he had gained management experience with various companies, he was a newcomer to the luxury-brand business. He began by learning about Louis

Vuitton's history and tradition. He was also keen to understand Japan, Louis Vuitton's first international market.

Carcelle understood that the brand's principles were built on the spirit of the Louis Vuitton family, its high level of craftsmanship, and the enthusiasm of its employees. By the time Marc Jacobs was appointed as Louis Vuitton's artistic director, Carcelle had acquired a profound understanding of the brand's essence. His leadership guided the success of Jacobs's creations for the business.

Often in times of success, one tends to hesitate before new challenges. Jacobs's success, however, proved that "fresh air from the outside provides invaluable strength."

A challenge in an unknown field

For Louis Vuitton, used to traditional products, the fashion business, in which each brand launches a new collection every season and focuses on topicality and the capabilities of its designers' capabilities, was a totally new universe.

Consequently, there was strong resistance within the company against its entry into the fashion business. Louis Vuitton had enjoyed a steady success in the manufacturing and marketing of leather goods. Entering the fashion business was a challenge in a completely unknown field, where product lines are renewed each season.

But the new management team eschewed conservatism and chose Marc Jacobs for the role of artistic director in 1997. The fact that a traditional French house had chosen a promising young American designer was received with amazement in the fashion industry. Louis Vuitton had suddenly advanced into the areas of prêt-à-porter and shoes.

Jacobs also made contributions to the existing product areas of bags and leather goods, creating a wide variety of fashionable and sophisticated bags, including the colorful "Monogram Vernis," the "Graffiti Series," and the "Monogram Mini." Introduced with prêt-à-porter at the biannual collections, they created a sensation. The combination of the Monogram designs, representing Louis Vuitton, and Marc Jacobs's fresh sensibility brought a modern-day renaissance to the brand.

The new bags provided many customers, familiar with the Vuitton tradition of durability and functionality, with the opportunity to rediscover the brand. They also brought Louis Vuitton a totally new clientele.

The synergistic effects of the merger

The huge expansion in our product lines required a larger space for product display. This led eventually to the opening of the first large "global stores."

Since the opening of the first global store on the Champs Élysées in Paris 1998, the number of global stores worldwide reached forty-nine in 2003. The effects were quite evident in Japan. Although Louis Vuitton Japan had enjoyed a steady growth in sales before Jacobs's appointment in 1997, the five years from 1997 to 2002 saw a huge sales increase of 64 billion yen ($533 million). This is almost three times the five-year sales increase of 22 billion yen ($193 million) from the previous five years, 1991 to 1996.

A complementary synergistic effect of the merger was also visible in the group's fashion brands. For example, Christian Dior had been losing its splendor and attraction in Japan because of a long term licensing contract with a Japanese textile manufacturer. Influenced by the success of Louis Vuitton in Japan, it decided to break off its license contract and devised a policy to enhance its imported product line of bags and clothes with better potential for steady sales. Along with the rejuvenation of the brand by the appointment of up-and-coming designer John Galliano, the success of the new series of bags became the driving force behind the huge advance of the new Christian Dior.

Within the LVMH conglomerate, fashionable Christian Dior and traditional Louis Vuitton created an excellent partnership, initiating and following new directions and proving that a good example of brand-business evolution will yield fruit.

The essence of luxury brands
Attempting to achieve perfection

After the bubble economy

The three years from 1987 (11.9 billion yen [$82 million] in sales) to 1990 (35.3 billion yen [$242 million] in sales) represent the peak of the crazy "bubble economy" for Louis Vuitton. In that short period, we experienced a nearly three-fold sales increase.

In 1991, however, year-on-year growth fell to 9 percent, and signs of a counter-reaction to the bubble economy became obvious in the second half of that year.

At the annual New Year's party for all employees, in early 1992, I spoke for an hour about the essence of luxury brands and businesses.

The effects of the collapse of the bubble economy were beginning to show in the entire Japanese economy, and some journalists even predicted the collapse of the "so-called brand businesses that rely on logos." As such, I was concerned that our employees might lose confidence.

What follows is a summary of my speech:

110

"I personally think that an annual growth of 8 to 12 percent is the limit for a luxury brand without compromising quality, taking into consideration expansion of production capacity and maintenance of the service support system. The growth rate of 40 to 50 percent achieved during the bubble economy completely exceeded this limit, and the achievement of such growth without major quality problems was exceptional. Compared with the 31 percent increase in 1990 and the 54 percent growth in 1989, the growth rate of 9 percent in 1991 may seem insignificant; however, a growth rate of 30 to 50 percent was abnormal for a business worth more than 10 billion yen ($74 million) without mass-production capabilities."

Requirements for a real brand

I also wanted to explain to the employees that Louis Vuitton did not fit into the theory of the "collapse of brand businesses." For the employees to understand that Louis Vuitton was a "real brand" among brands, I outlined the six requirements for a real brand:

1. A long history
2. Consistent tradition
3. Unique technology and know-how

4. A unique philosophy

5. Unique aesthetic values

6. High quality and quality assurance

I also said that only a brand that fulfills these six requirements deserves to be called a real brand. At the end of my speech, I introduced the keywords for 1992: history, tradition, technology, philosophy, aesthetic values, and quality assurance.

Since then, I have always presented keywords in my New Year's speech to the employees. With the increase in the number of employees, however, it has become impossible to hold a New Year's party. I now deliver my message by video at the beginning of each year.

1993: Passion

When asked about the difference between Louis Vuitton and other companies, without hesitation I always say "passion." I am referring to our employees' passion for Louis Vuitton products and for the brand.

I also tell all the new employees that without passion, they are wasting their time with us. Even the greatest strategies will fail without the right mindset in the people who carry them out.

1994: 365 and 9.9

Shortly after beginning our activities in Japan, during a visit to the president of a chain of department stores to offer my New Year's greetings, he offered the following encouraging comment on Louis Vuitton: "When I was younger, my senior associate in a department store taught me that the key to success in the department store business lay in the change of the seasons.

"In other words, the turn of the seasons was the best opportunity to sell new products to customers. However, Mr. Hata, my ideas totally changed after getting to know Louis Vuitton. Louis Vuitton products sell throughout the year, regardless of the season."

The keyword "365" resulted from this experience. It conveys the message that a real brand must have the merchandising ability to sell products every day of the year, regardless of the season, the fashion trends, or the times.

The keyword "9.9" originates from a comment by Shiseido's then president, Yoshiharu Fukuhara, when we invited him to our factory in Asnières, on the outskirts of Paris. There he saw the manual production process of trunks by craftsmen that has taken place for more than 100 years. In a conversation with mathematician Tsuyoshi Mori, he said, "In a 100-meter dash, the difference between a sprinter who takes 10 seconds and another one who takes 9.9 seconds is only 0.1 second. But that 0.1 second can mean winning or losing the race. The value of things is like that. This slight difference in the end makes a great difference."

This 0.1 second difference is amplified beyond our imagination. If we say 11 seconds are acceptable, we will never exert ourselves to pursue the ultimate value.

The same applies to the brand business. Only the best brands can deliver absolute value, in addition to unique products. Therefore, the mentality to pursue the last 0.1 second is very important in the brand business. A desire to achieve perfection is indispensable. There is no perfect thing in this world. There is also no perfect person or perfect product. It is very important, however, to make the effort to achieve perfection.

Just like the 100-meter sprinters exert themselves to eliminate that last 0.1 second, a brand must persistently strive to create perfect products and service. Neglecting such efforts means giving up the ideal of becoming a real brand. The keyword "9.9" was derived from this idea.

1995: Inevitability and Creativity
Our new employees, as well as journalists, often ask the question, "Will Louis Vuitton keep growing in sales as it has done in past years?" My reply to this question was

inspired by my reading of *The End of History and the Last Man* by Francis Fukuyama.

A third-generation Japanese-American sociologist, Fukuyama predicted the demise of the Soviet Union in his dissertation and later became famous. After the Soviet Union actually collapsed, his dissertation was published as a book in 1992. His prediction was based on the Hegelian theory of the human "desire for cognition"—that is, the desire to be recognized by others, to be accepted as a unique individual different from others. Familiar examples include the desire to live in a unique house, to wear a distinctive outfit, or to express one's opinion freely.

In the Soviet Union at the time, basic living standards for survival were satisfied. Nevertheless, the desire for cognition, which naturally follows survival, didn't exist in that political, social, and economic structure.

Fukuyama predicted that such a system would soon collapse. Paraphrasing Hegel, he wrote: "People long for what others have, and desire even more what they don't have." This is a great insight into the nature of man. I feel that these words were the reason for which Louis Vuitton would continue to grow in sales—because behind this growth is the inevitable nature of man. In fact, this nature, proposed by Hegel, endorsed my theory that people naturally long for high quality. It may sound like a bold conclusion, but Louis Vuitton need not worry about sales decreases as long as we address our customers' needs.

1996: Honesty and Truth

The Corporate Charter—our mission statement—was published in the April 1990 edition of the internal newsletter issued by Louis Vuitton Malletier. In it, the concepts of honesty and truth were at the top of the list, followed by other attributes such as durability, functionality, and unique materials.

These words made such a long-lasting impression on me that I eventually made them the keywords for 1996. In the world of luxury brands, it is sometimes hard to manage success. Honesty and truth, however, are the most important attributes in this industry. In 1996 we got back on the track of growth after the collapse of the bubble economy and achieved sales of 60 billion yen ($533 million). It was especially important for us to value honesty and truth above all else at that time.

1997: Mythologizing Our Service

In 1997 sales exceeded 70 billion yen ($573 million), store numbers reached thirty-eight, and the number of employees increased to 438. The previous year had been especially eventful.

The Seven Designers Series had been launched to commemorate the 100th anniversary of the Monogram canvas, and the *damier* canvas had been revived for the first time in 100 years. I felt then the need to focus on service, and we embarked on a company-wide program to improve service with the slogan "Mythologizing our service." Details of the program for customer-service improvements that were implemented at the time can be found in Chapter 5 (*Mythologizing our service*).

1998: The challenge to innovate

In 1998 Louis Vuitton Japan celebrated its 20th anniversary. It was also the year Marc Jacobs's first collection was launched.

The introduction of fashion product lines in the 145th year of Louis Vuitton's history was a milestone for the brand, making 1998 the year of "the challenge to innovate." Having joined the LVMH group, where many fashion brands coexist, made the fashion industry more familiar to Louis Vuitton Japan. Nevertheless, the launch of prêt-à-porter and shoes at the first global store in Japan (the Shinsaibashi store in Osaka) was a great challenge. The product launch meant adding seasonal fashion items to the regular items, which were unaffected by season or fashion trend. We had to take on new challenges with new ideas, without conforming to the success and business thinking of the past.

This would be true in all areas: sales and promotional activities, human resource development, and inventory control. So at the beginning of the year, I addressed all employees and said, "New challenges always involve a risk. With the success of our principal business, it is now the time to take up new challenges. We will not take a passive attitude toward risk-taking."

1999: Clear Vision, Honest Business, Patience, and Perseverance

People frequently ask, "What is the secret of Louis Vuitton's success?" My answer is always the same: "There is no secret. We simply do what we have to do, and we do it with honesty."

There is no easy path to success, and to give a complete answer to this question would take hours. At the end of the millennium, however, I felt obliged to convey to our employees the essential elements for success as a real brand. That is why I delivered this key message: "Work with perseverance, passion and honesty, sustained by a clear vision and philosophy."

2000: Devotion and Commitment

Together with the keywords "passion" for 1993 and "9.9" for 1994, I wanted to remind employees that to work for a brand, they must adopt a mentality characterized by the spirit of devotion and commitment.

2001-2002: Sensibility and conviction"

With the arrival of the 21st century, large corporations that were once considered invincible went bankrupt or experienced huge losses. I began to feel that the industrial infrastructure and "efficiency-first" policies based on standardized mass production were about to reach their limit.

Such an infrastructure was the basis of the rapid economic growth of post–World War II Japan. Nevertheless, it must be recognized that this efficiency-first business process contributed to improved living standards through mass production of quality products and marketing at reasonable prices is crucial. Today, however, with high labor costs in Japan, this process is no longer sufficient to win the competition against developing countries. We need to offer an added value that surpasses efficiency. Added value can't be expressed in numbers. It is something that appeals to people's sensibility, and that is the key to success in the luxury-business world. I wanted to convey the importance of enhancing sensibility to all employees.

The other key word, "conviction," means "belief" as well, but belief in a sense that implies being passionate. I was trying to explain that a person in the brand business must have "conviction" as well as "passion" (the keyword for 1993).

I have come to understand that the greatest scientific inventors, including the recent Japanese Nobel Prize winners and the most successful businesspeople, have in common their perseverance and their conviction.

Thomas Edison once said: "Great inventions come from 99 percent hard work and 1 percent inspiration." I think 99 percent of hard work is equal to awareness of problems.

If you remain conscious of problems, solutions are born out of inspiration. To find out more about the power of "belief," I recommend the following books: *The Magic of Believing*, by Claude M. Bristol, and *The Principles of Creation*, by Haruo Uehara

2003: Individuality and creativity

I always give a speech to new employees on their first day with us—twice a month I speak to a group of 20 to 30 people. I want them to understand the philosophy and values of the Louis Vuitton brand from the very start. I always introduce the keywords of the current year.

The keywords for 2003 were "individuality" and "creativity." In my estimation, the 21st century will be the century of individuality, and this individuality will require creativity. Political power will shift from factions to individual politicians, who will have to demonstrate vision and leadership.

In the business world, it is original, unique products that are desired. People with their own opinions and the ability to establish original ideas will be valued. As we move from the group-oriented era to individualism, the individual will need creativity.

Since the Meiji Restoration, Japan has opted for the efficient method of "imitation" in order to catch up with the Western world. Education is the best example: the educational system has leaned towards memorization, and as result, Japanese people have neglected to think for themselves.

As we have caught up with the West, the memoriza-tion-based educational system and imitation-based busi-ness models are no longer effective. The 21st century will be an era of creativity. To achieve growth or to succeed in career development, both businesses and individuals will need creativity. Looking back, I can say that a real brand never wastes time copying others. What is important is to constantly pursue new business models, with flexibility and creative ideas, from product development through to the distribution process.

Toward an era of global strength

With the arrival of the 21st century, the brand business has entered an era of global strength. It is easier to understand the meaning of global strength if we look at the development pattern of Louis Vuitton as a brand business.

1854–1976: Brand establishment and operation to its limit as a family business

1977: Introduction of professional management

1978: Full-scale entry into the international market

1984: Listing of the company's stock

1987: Merger with companies of different sectors and formation of a group

1998: Entry into new fields of business

2000: Development and expansion of a worldwide store network

2002: Building of large-scale production and distribution systems

2003: Expansion of global customer service

The transition from product-based competition to selling-power competition

As Louis Vuitton illustrates, a luxury brand starts with unique, high-quality products based on the craftsmanship and technique of the company. Typically, at first the business is operated by the founder's family. The period from brand establishment to the introduction of external professional management is the era of product and design-centered competition.

The history, tradition, and skills accrued over the years are the foundation of the brand and its business. By protecting such values, the brand is recognized as a unique entity in the market.

When the brand enters the international market, however, those values are not enough to succeed against the competition. It is now faced with selling power competition—the establishment of a sales network. A competition of quantity develops as well, in which the number and scale of the marketing points, such as stores, becomes important. At the same time, or soon after, the brand shifts to a competition of quality. Here "quality" doesn't mean product quality but quality of sales, that is quality of service.

The quality of the sales staff is the most important element in a competition of quality. It takes time to achieve this goal, because good personnel cannot be developed in a day.

The company's reputation and reliability are crucial elements in the recruitment of good personnel. Louis Vuitton Japan has recently moved up in popularity among college graduates looking for potential employers.

In the latest survey, it ranks among the top 40 (and number one among foreign-affiliated companies). In the specialty retail industry, we moved from the 17th position in 2002 to number one in 2003. Employment is just the beginning, however. Other important issues include education, training, the provision of a career path, and promotion motivation.

Louis Vuitton has domestic and international training programs for the employees of our stores, which include a visit to the head office in Paris and to the museum and factory in Asnières. More than 250 Japanese employees participate annually in our training program in Paris.

Operational competency to support market expansion
With more than 30 stores and sales figures of 30 to 40 billion yen (306 million dollars to 368 million dollars), efficient product supply is crucial. At this point, it becomes necessary to put into place Supply Chain

Management, or SCM. SCM is a management method the goal of which to eliminate redundant stock and improve cash flow by promoting the efficiency of a process that involves the procurement of materials, manufacturing, distribution, and the delivery of products to customers.

It may be easy to recognize issues of production capacity—that is, production plans based on each product's projected sales and the delivery of products to market according to certain priorities. But it is not an easy task to establish an efficient system. The collection of daily sales data from each store may not be a big issue. Forecasting each product's sales, however, is very difficult. When forecasting a new product's sales, sometimes it is necessary to depend on the "hunches" of the frontline staff, the marketing and merchandising staff, and the senior management staff.

In addition, the more products are sold, the more important the after-sales service becomes. The establishment of our repair service system (explained in Chapter 5) was the first step toward improving this service.

Requirements for the brands of the future
I hope that these examples of the concept of global

strength have made it easier to understand that the brand business has shifted from competition of product quality and design to global-strength competition.

The following are eight elements for global strength that the brands of the future will require:

1. Creativity and planning ability for product development
2. Ability to expand, develop, control, and manage a sales network
3. Ability to provide global service to satisfy customers
4. Ability to evolve, while maintaining consistency PR and marketing
5. Technical innovation, and the development of information technology able to support efficient production and logistics
6. Ability to recruit and train competent personnel
7. Ability to procure funds
8. Maintenance of the company's reputation and the trust of society

Today's society keeps changing under a flood of information. New products constantly emerge and disappear. To be recognized as a brand that transcends time, place, and culture, these eight elements are indispensable.

The brand name and the logo are not what matters. What matters are the creative abilities and management capabilities behind them. The brand business encompasses the essence of all businesses.

I was born and raised in Kochi (a town in Shikoku, previously called Tosa) near the Harimaya Bridge. I was 8 years old when World War II ended. The changes in the social system that followed transformed my daily life.

Western culture, particularly American-style material affluence, had begun began to spread, and, I felt the impact of these changes where I lived. Western movies became more popular than Japanese ones; Western classical and pop music could be heard everywhere.

As an ordinary boy, I was fascinated by such American affluence. I loved the movies most. I began making great efforts to learn English to understand them without relying on subtitles. I wanted to be a film critic, or rather an literary critic like Hideo Kobayashi. These were my teenage dreams.

But I was born into a family of merchants. My father had very sharp business acumen. He advised me to study economics, because he thought that only extremely gifted people could make a living as critics. That is how I ended up at the faculty of economics of Keio University after graduating from Tosa High School. Upon graduation from Keio in 1961, I went to America to continue my studies, following the advice of my brother-in-law, architect Masayoshi Yendo.

After one year of intensive English practice at the University of California at Berkeley, I entered the Amos Tuck School of Business Administration at Dartmouth College in New Hampshire.

The foundations of my way of thinking

What I learned from Professor J. B. Quinn in the very first course I attended at Amos Tuck has become the foundation of my way of thinking.

I had to make a presentation before the class. I had read the many documents that were handed to us the day before, and I had noted the key points that needed to be addressed. During my presentation, Professor Quinn, who had been quietly listening, turned to me and said, "Mr. Hata, I'd like to know what you think about the text. Everyone knows what the text is about; you don't need to explain it. What I want you to do is to make an analysis and raise points."

Despite my hard work, the presentation was a complete disaster. But this experience left a strong impression on me. My ways of doing and thinking had been flatly rejected. This experience made me reconsider the real meaning of thinking: to think with one's own head; to derive and analyze different ideas from other people and to draw conclusions from them; and to put those conclusions into practice believing in what you are doing.

This lesson helped me learn how to think and solve problems. It is something I later developed in my job as a consultant and that was also very useful when I had to work out a strategy for Louis Vuitton's debut in Japan.

The story of a brand

In the past, many people told me that I should write a book. I declined each time, however, because the time was not right. I decided to write this book, however, on the 25th anniversary of Louis Vuitton Japan because I wanted to explain my views on brands by drawing on my own experience.

Finally, I want to say that what I have achieved is not just the result of my own efforts. I have been blessed with many capable employees, friends, and assistants. These employees, who are now directors or advisers, have shared my joys and sorrows. We sometimes quarreled over business policy, but they have always supported and encouraged me. Without them, Louis Vuitton Japan wouldn't be what it is today. I would like to take this opportunity to express my deep gratitude to all the people who have shown me their support and cooperation in many ways.

Omotesando, December 2003

KYOJIRO HATA

In December 2003 I published my first book with Nihon Keizai Shimbun, Inc. (a major Japanese economic newspaper corporation), to commemorate the 25th anniversary of Louis Vuitton in Japan. At that time, I did not envisage publishing French or English versions of my book.

With the warm encouragement of my colleagues at Louis Vuitton, as well as some other LVMH Group companies, I started to look into the possibility of the venture.

First I checked with a friend of mine working with a large French publishing company in Japan. The reaction was not positive, but he suggested that I contact Assouline.

Coincidentally, several months earlier, I'd had an opportunity to meet for the first time Prosper and Martine Assouline on a flight from Paris to Tokyo and had the pleasure of accompanying them to our Omotesando store the following day.

Therefore, I knew Assouline's name, but I had the impression that they specialized in a particular type of beautiful and luxury books.

To make a long story short, to my pleasant surprise, Mr. Assouline expressed his interest in publishing my book not only in French but also in English. After that, everything went very quickly as I dealt directly with Mr. and Mrs. Assouline, who are the final decision makers at Assouline.

I would like to take this opportunity to express my sincere appreciation to them for taking the risk of publishing a book such as mine.

In closing, I would like to express my sincere thanks to the many people who assisted me in promoting the publication of this book, particularly, Mr. Emmanuel Prat, president and representative director of LVMH K.K., and my assistant, Ms. Mayumi Kohda.

KYOJIRO HATA

Photographic credits